Voices Outside The Stadium:

Face to Face with Human Trafficking Outside Major Sporting Events 2015 - 2018

Skyway Railroad

Compiled by Kaitrin E. Valencia, Esq.

Skyway Railroad
PO BOX 48
Eads, Tennessee 38002
www.skywayrailroad.org
Skywayrailroad48@gmail.com

Cover design: Imelda Valencia Cuevas

ISBN-13: 978-1-7323597-0-3

DEDICATION

Voices Outside the Stadium is dedicated to all the
courageous children, women, and men who are trafficked
at major sporting events and the relentless volunteers, organizations,
and law enforcement who reach, rescue, and restore them.

It is also dedicated to Casey, the first trafficked woman who
flew to freedom on the Skyway.
She remains one of the bravest women we know.

CONTENTS

ACKNOWLEDGMENTS

Voices Outside the Stadium is a collaborative publication written by our volunteers and compiled and edited by Kaitrin Valencia.

Contributing reflections were provided by the following volunteers who served and loved tenaciously: Marie Birr, Matthew Durrbeck, Jennifer Dybala, Yesenia Hagstrom, Susan Hartman, Elizabeth Kruse, Amanda McCoy, Lisette Paez, Dillon Patterson, Bailey Schuchard, Noelani Torres, Kaitrin Valencia, and Joseph Wynkoop.

Thank you, modern-day abolitionists, for helping these voices be heard outside the stadium! This book project would not be possible without you.

Thank you to Imelda Valencia Cuevas for designing an incredible book cover that captures what we encounter each year conducting outreach at the national football championship game.

Thank you to the many ministries who partner with us nationwide every year (too many to name) and the volunteers who consistently help us reach and restore those we contact. We especially appreciate Butterfly Effect for donating 20% of every T-shirt sale to help with publishing costs. To purchase a "Person Not Possession" shirt visit: www.butterflyeffects.us.

A huge thank you to New Life Covenant Church in Chicago and Chicago Masters Commission (Pastors Anders and Yesenia Hagstrom) who send students every year to serve as the backbone behind this mission trip. For more information about becoming a student visit: www.chicagomc.org.

Lastly, we thank the Father, Jesus, and the Holy Spirit who protects us and provides provision and healing to survivors, pimps, and johns.

All glory goes to God!

CHAPTER 1
SETTING THE STAGE

Human trafficking is an epidemic that's plagued our society for centuries. The largest single human trafficking venues occur whenever and wherever major sporting events take place. Thousands of male fans fly into the hosting cities where, unfortunately, a high demand for escort services is created. To meet these demands, thousands of girls, boys, women, and men are flown into the hosting venue and trafficked – sold – at these sporting events.

Each year, fans can be heard shouting and screaming for their respective team inside the stadium. However, there are other shouts and screams outside the stadium that the world never hears. They are our missing, abused and neglected children, our abandoned women, our vulnerable boys, and men.

The Skyway Railroad is a national nonprofit that partners each year with other organizations, task forces, and local, state, and federal law enforcement to reach, rescue, and place those trafficked the week of the professional football championship game in the U.S. The final game is held in a different city every year and we have volunteers on the ground making sure those being trafficked are reached and have access to help if they are ready to escape.

Some try to cover up this reality of thousands being trafficked the week of the game because it brings bad publicity. They claim it's a myth. However, as individuals who've been to these national football final games since 2015, we can attest these voices are real and in desperate pain and fear.

Each one has a name. Their voices aren't a myth. We have met them. We have flown to the games on packed planes, surrounded by them. We have prayed with them in strip clubs, brothels, and on the streets. We have cried with them. We have fed and clothed them. We have bound up literal wounds. We have helped them get back home or to a permanent safe house for human trafficking survivors. We have left with their mascara stains on our shirts after praying for them with their heads buried in our chests out of sheer desperation.

This publication is our meager attempt to shout their voices outside the stadiums so you can hear their reality in the places we visit them: hotels, massage parlors (also called brothels), strip clubs, bus and train stations, airport terminals, truck stops, and on the streets in what are called "tracks" (streets known for trafficking). They've been silenced too long. But now, we declare "No more."

Most of our interactions with victims are brief, because they are being watched and time is money. We never want our efforts to put anyone in danger. Yet, as you will see, every interaction (even if brief) is power-packed in the way only God can accomplish. We offer prayer to each individual and provide some type of "takeaway" with our hotline number if they want resources, prayer, or help to escape the industry. Takeaways include roses, carnations, gift bags, and in cold venues, packs of tissue.

Throughout the week our volunteers write their experience of support and rescue, which now fill these pages. The reflections are written in each volunteer's words, have a title, and end with a prompt for you to stop and pray for those touched in the specific encounter. While the breaks for prayer may feel repetitive, every interaction is connected to actual people. We believe your prayers have the power to break yokes and chains.

If read straight through, this book can be finished in one sitting as an "easy" read. However, we pray this will be one of the most challenging books you read because it represents actual encounters and actual people. We ask for you to not gloss quickly over each reflection but instead pause and invade the heavenly realm with your powerful intercession.

Our goal in publishing these stories is twofold: (1) to bring awareness to the atrocities in human trafficking by giving the marginalized a voice; and (2) for all book proceeds to help us reach these same desperate voices the following year. One hundred percent of the proceeds goes to the outreach. Thank you for the investment made when you purchased this book, which will help us continue serving and saving lives. If you want more information about our organization, please visit www.skywayrailroad.org.

As a disclaimer, some of these pages are filled with explicit material that is reality to so many. We want to avoid any content being a trigger for anyone struggling with pornography or other sexual sins. Please guard your mind and your heart as you read through these reflections.

Thank you for supporting these voices today, and for helping us reach next year's voices who are all too often misunderstood and silenced.

CHAPTER 2
BOYS TRAPPED AS MEN

Whenever you hear about sex trafficking, the common belief is that only women and girls are trafficked or only men are pimps. No. Boys and men are also trafficked and women (called madams and bottoms) also traffick individuals. We don't minister only to the people being trafficked. We also have men on our team who minister to the men: the johns (another name for customers purchasing sex), the pimps, and men/boys being trafficked. There are "tracks" (areas known for prostitution) where we encounter transgender men and boys and we have also ministered during sporting event outreaches at gay male strip clubs. These venues are reached by our male volunteers.

Many times we are asked, "Are you safe doing this work?" We don't operate in fear because we know from the Bible that fear is not from God (2 Timothy 1:7). We will not give pimps or the enemy the power of our fear. Instead, we operate with wisdom. We never put ourselves or our volunteers in compromising or dangerous positions. Our team's safety is our top priority.

All of our volunteers are trained and we use strictly designed protocols, measures, and techniques to ensure everyone's safety. And believe it or not, many pimps are extremely receptive when our Holy Spirit-filled teams approach. They—as well as the johns—are hurting and also need Jesus. They're addicted and bound and need freedom too. Think of it this way: if God can transform one pimp, this will impact and reach all the girls he is exploiting or will exploit. We therefore place high value on reaching and ministering to the men.

The following are just a few encounters we've had with men during our outreach the week of this major football sporting event.

Smoke Jesus?

We were in San Francisco. My favorite childhood football team was playing and had just won the championship game! All week during outreach I had gear from my team and was trash-talking wherever and whenever I could. When we won the big game, the streets were wild with fans displaying the same gear and cheering the same sentiments.

As I stood outside a strip club on our outreach itinerary, a young college kid from Denver (we'll call him Patrick) was celebrating this same team's victory in the streets. Patrick had just left the strip club and, from the looks of it, came outside to join the celebratory festivities. To say he was inebriated is an understatement. He could barely walk.

When I encountered Patrick, he saw my common jersey and we began high-fiving and cheering when the following interaction took place:

> Patrick: "You smoke weed?"
> Me (in an instantaneous response as we are high-fiving): "No, I smoke Jesus!"
> BAM, he gets a high five.
> Patrick: "I smoke Him too."
> Me: "You can't smoke both, bro."
> Long silence and pause.
> Me: "Can we pray for you real quick?"

Patrick and his friends gathered around us and we huddled in a circle with him barely able to stand. The Holy Spirit led me in a quick prayer that sounded like something to this effect:

> "God, I thank You for this young man and his friends. I thank You for his life that is filled with such future purpose. I pray when he goes back to that strip club and he looks at the girl dancing on the pole, that he sees the face of his future daughter, his future wife. In Jesus' name, amen."

Patrick opened his eyes in utter shock and disbelief, tears streaming down his face. He squinted his eyes, jerked his head back and forth as if to try and focus, looked at his friend, and said, "Man, I'm outta here. I'm going home." He climbed into a taxi and didn't go back into that strip club. Hallelujah!

Please, stop and pray for this young man who was literally young enough to be my son.

Praying Grandma

Our team was walking the streets of San Francisco, 2016, with roses. We gave these to girls walking the area who appeared to be "working." Each flower had a card attached with information to call for help.

We came to a group of four or five girls of different races who were all standing in front of a liquor store. There was a male (we'll call him Max) in the middle of them, with half of the girls on one side and half on his other side. Our volunteers tried going to each of the girls individually to give them a rose, but they avoided eye contact with us. They kept looking back at Max, who looked as tough as nails.

I pushed my way through everyone in the group, laid my hand on Max's chest, and boldly—through the prompting of the Holy Spirit— said, "You have a praying grandma!"

His jaw, which was tense when we approached, immediately began to quiver. Tears welled up and streamed down his face. When the Holy Spirit smacks you in your head and heart, the whole world stops. It doesn't matter who's looking.

I began prophetically speaking life into Max:

> "You were raised in church! You know the Word of God! Your grandma is praying for you right now. Instead of leading these girls to darkness, you are called to lead them to the throne of God and the throne of grace."

Max allowed us to pray with him and now all the girls joined. Hallelujah! Mid-prayer, another guy came from around the corner where he'd been standing, broke the circle of held hands, and joined in the prayer. Without question, the Holy Spirit left Max and all those in the big circle outside that corner liquor store different from how we found him.

Since that encounter, I often think of Max and say a prayer for him. Only heaven will tell the impact that this three-to-five-minute interaction had on this man and all those he may have enslaved in the future had we not encountered him.

Would you stop right now and pray for this young man and his warrior grandmother? God knows his real name and God knows his needs. I can't wait to see him face-to-face in heaven!

Lustful Married Eyes

Phoenix, Arizona, 2015. We were given access to a strip club with a huge wide-open space and lounge chairs everywhere. Large end tables were filled with drinks, and hundreds of men and women worked the whole room. Money covered the floor. We were literally stepping on dollar bills under our feet, hearing the sound of crunching as we walked.

We had gift bags with small items in each and our standard business card. I had 15 to 20 looped around my fingers and was making my way through the room giving them to women who were walking from one encounter to another, wearing little to no clothes.

You could feel the heaviness in the room. It was smoky, dark, and filled with the spirit of lust. Everywhere we looked men were getting lap dances and fervently touching the women sprawled on top of them. It was like an open room full of orgies, in real life, right in front of us. I'd never seen anything like it, but we had to act completely normal.

As long as I live I will never forget one of the man's face. He was receiving a lap dance, his hands were on the woman's thighs rubbing up and down, and he had a wedding ring on his left hand. My heart sank for him, his wife, and who knows, maybe children. In fact, as I began paying more attention, I saw that most of the men in the room also wore wedding rings.

Yes, you may be reading this and have negative thoughts towards these men and these behaviors. Trust me, disgust was my initial reaction. But the more I've done outreach, the more the Holy Spirit has checked my disgust and replaced it with an open heart.

Jesus loves these men, and we are called to pray for their healing and deliverance as well. Without them and the demand they create, there would be no need for the services rendered by the girls. But the sad reality is for every girl we rescue, the trafficker/industry will just replace her if there continues to be a demand for the services.

This may sound insensitive, but basic business principles show if you want to put someone out of business, you eliminate the demand for the product. If we want to effectively end human trafficking we must, therefore, end the demand for purchased sex. And to start, we must believe that no one is beyond the powerful redemption of Jesus. So ministering to the men bound in captivity is also our mission during outreaches.

As I walked around this club praying, almost in a trance, one girl was exiting a lap dance and I handed her a bag. She looked at me and half smiled. I asked her if I could pray for her, which seemed to ground her deeper than her motion of stretching out her hand to grab the gift bag I offered.

At that moment, with no top on but with the opportunity for prayer, she fell into my arms and buried her face in my shoulder. We prayed together. After we were done, black mascara streamed down her face and the remnants covered my shirt where she'd rested her head during our brief prayer. I spoke life into her and quickly moved on because I didn't want her to get in trouble.

I pray I never get used to these encounters and environments. My desire is that God will greatly move my spirit to remember and offer prayer for years to come for every person I've interacted with.

Would you soften your heart for the men bound in lust and pray for them right now, and for this one girl who buried herself in my chest and wept, just to be released back into calloused, exploitative, dangerous arms?

Pastor Intercepted

Houston, Texas, 2017, outside of a strip club. We always bring men with us on outreach. They never go inside the strip clubs (for obvious reasons) and we have them stand outside at angles where they cannot see anything when the doors swing open. We usually have baked goods with Scripture attached for our male volunteers to offer and minister to the bouncers as they stand and interact with men outside.

Here's a divine account of one interaction outside a strip club: One of our male team members was in the parking lot of one of the clubs we were visiting. He was performing his "watcher" role when a guy asked him, "Do you know the cover charge to get in here?" Our team member (who happened to be one of the pastors leading our team) said, "No, I'm just here trying to prevent human trafficking."

As the conversation continued, the pastor on our team felt led to ask if he could pray for this gentleman. The guy said, "Fine, pray for me." After the prayer our pastor said to the guy, "Going to one of these places doesn't seem like you. You seem very uncomfortable here." The patron then revealed that this was his first time considering going to "one of these clubs," and he was unsure about going in. The man revealed he used to be a youth pastor but stepped down because he was struggling with pornography. Going to the strip club seemed like a logical "next step."

Our team member encouraged him, spoke life into him, and offered himself as an accountability partner. They exchanged numbers and the intercepted former youth pastor agreed that going inside was not the correct next step.

WOW! God, at that specific point in time, at that specific place, with that specific team from miles away, with one of our pastors, met His prodigal son before he took a step further into a dark addiction.

Saints, make this a stopping point and engage your prayer for every pastor and every person in ministry—male and female—who struggles with pornography, including the man we intercepted. This addiction is not only keeping so many of God's children bound in pain, it's also the on-ramp for many other sexual sins.

CHAPTER 3
STRIP CLUB OUTREACH

You may ask why we go to strip clubs to reach girls who are being trafficked. Many of the clubs are coordinated locally, regionally, and nationally. The owners take girls across state lines to events, parties, and even other strip clubs to make money off the services they render. We've also learned from the women that they're expected to reach a "quota" each night for how many lap dances they perform. If they don't meet the quota for the night, the strip club keeps all their proceeds.

But when they do meet the quota, the women must pay a fee to the strip club for each lap dance they perform. How is this not sexual exploitation? The girls are also exposed to much coercion, manipulation, and darkness while working in these clubs.

Following are the words of one volunteer who conducted strip club outreach in Phoenix, 2015, during the week of the football championship game:

As I walked into the strip club I saw so much money. People were walking on what seemed to be a carpet made of dollar bills. There were women in the dressing rooms with counting stacks and stacks of money with who appeared to be the madam.

The later the night got, the more crowded the clubs. We were generally not allowed to interrupt women "on the floor" and had to go into the dressing rooms where we would briefly stop and pray with the women and give them gifts. During one stop at around 2 in the morning, the club was so packed that we could barely walk in the dressing room. There were probably more than 200 naked girls in the back, with everyone literally squeezing by each other. The girls were lathering their bodies with oil for when they danced on the poles. Because there were so many girls that night, I left with oil all over my arms and clothes from the tight corridors.

Holy warriors, take a moment to pray for that roomful of girls, covered in oil and slipping past help to a potentially dark fate. They, too, are worthy of the joy and cleansing brought by the love of Jesus.

Unlikely Frequenters

Our outreach teams went to local brothels, massage parlors, strip clubs, nightclubs, hotel bars, casinos, and downtown streets. Before this outreach, I would've thought: "What in the world am I doing in those places?" Well, as crazy as it sounds, we did ministry there. It was a huge blessing to show them we cared and were there for them. I learned in my interactions how women may sometimes start down this path as a "choice," working at a strip club job. But it's in those same situations where they end up trapped and later forced into providing other services.

At the strip clubs, I couldn't go in because I wasn't yet 21. So the older women in our group went in and spoke with those "working," to be love to them, and hear their story. We also handed out care packages.

At the nightclubs, hotel bars, and casinos, we were extra eyes to scout for any situations where it looked like trafficking was taking place. It was so heartbreaking because if the victims we saw weren't minors, there wasn't much we could do about it. We'd still hand out tissues wherever fitting, mostly leaving them in the bathrooms. But it hurt to know they were so close to our help, yet so far. At times I just wanted to scream, and at others, I wanted to break down and cry. So much pain and darkness these women were experiencing...so much.

We also had a team talk with the women on the downtown streets who gave roses to those they encountered. It was honestly so cold, it was sickening to know the pimps made these women stand outside until they made a certain amount of money. These precious women were treated like meat and it broke my heart so painfully.

During every encounter we had, we asked if we could pray for them and they couldn't believe it. People have only ever wanted things from them, so for us to give them something and care for them without conditions, they were incredibly thankful.

Now, share your prayer for God's grace on behalf of those women. The Holy Spirit knows who needs intervention and light, and is awaiting your voice to join the chorus of angels.

Eating My Own Words

"I've got this!" has always been a phrase I've used in school, work, and even on the trip I took in 2018 to Minneapolis, just a few hours from where I lived. One night we were walking into a strip club to give roses to the girls working and pray with them. The only words that came to my mind were: "I've got this." Yes, I was terrified, but I knew I wasn't going in alone.

Our team went backstage and started talking to the girls in their dressing rooms. One particular girl sitting alone in the corner of the dressing room grabbed my attention. I walked up to her and started the conversation by complimenting her nails. As the conversation progressed, I asked her where she was from and she said she just flew into town that day for the sporting event. That's as far as the answer went.

I asked her if there was anything that I could pray for her about and she used my own words on me: "I've got this." I asked what she meant by that and she responded that she had herself and she had it together. As we were leaving all I could think about was how that one phrase could mask someone's situation, pain, and longing for love. One phrase could make or break a relationship, build up or tear down walls, or could bring restoration to someone in need.

Now, it's your turn. You got this. Pray for that woman, and all the others we encountered who still ache for the blessings of our Lord.

Breaking Through The Curtain

San Francisco, California, 2016. We went to a strip club one night but we weren't granted access by the manager, who was very bitter. He sneered that the girls were "all busy giving lap dances," and so we couldn't enter. There was a Dutch door (one in which the lower and upper part can be opened separately) at the entrance to the establishment. On the other side of this Dutch door was a curtain blocking the stage and most of what was going on inside. We could see the bar and the women working behind the bar, which was in earshot range from where we were standing at the entrance.

The female bartender—who wore almost no clothes—smiled at us (obviously having heard the explanation of why we were there) and she was counting a stack of money. The manager agreed to let us leave the gift bags for the girls who were working and when we asked how many girls there were, he told us "11." This was the smallest group of girls we had encountered the entire trip.

Two of the girls who overheard our conversation came barging through the curtain and fell into our arms over the top of the Dutch door in total appreciation of our kind gesture. We were able to pray for them and when we finished, one said we were going to make her cry. They both talked about how they "go to church together."

As we left there and I thought of those girls tearing through that protective curtain, I couldn't help but think about how when Jesus died on the cross the veil (curtain) was torn, giving us complete access to the Holy of Holies.

Pause now, and say a power-packed prayer for these two women, the angry manager, and every girl in that small but extremely dark establishment.

52 and Living Out of a Car

After going to a strip club and ministering to women, we were in the parking lot sitting in our van and praying for each encounter we'd just had inside. Our driver, a young Master's Commission student, motioned to a parked car where two men sat with a woman. The men proceeded to leave the car and the woman stayed in it.

Bingo!

Our team jumped out of our van, walked over to the car to give the woman a rose and offer prayer. We learned she was 52 years old, and she shared how it had become too expensive to live in San Francisco (where we were conducting outreach). She was forced to sell her condo, tried moving to another state, but said that "didn't work out" so she came back to San Francisco.

All of her belongings, everything she owned, was in this car in which she was living. She described feeling tired and wanted out. She'd begun using drugs and admitted if she came with us right then, she'd need to detox. Even though she was tired, she unfortunately wasn't ready. She didn't come with us.

We prayed for her, then watched her get out of the car and change into her clothes right there in the parking lot to go to work at the strip club. Her car was her home and the street was her changing room at that particular moment in time.

Place your finger in your book right now to hold this spot and begin to intercede for this 52-year-old homeless and drug-addicted woman working at a strip club.

On Her Way Out

We were being escorted to the dressing room of a strip club in Minneapolis, Minnesota, 2018. As soon as I walked through the doors I stopped to give a woman a gift bag and a hug. She appeared really excited and said she still had the bracelet we'd given her. I explained we were a different outreach group and it was obvious these girls had another ministry who came in frequently to minister to them and they mistook us for them.

She was so bubbly and appreciative. She leaned in and whispered in my ear, "This is my last week. I'm quitting next week because I got a job at a credit card company."

My heart pounded so hard with excitement, it was about to leap out of my chest. I gave her the biggest high five I think I have ever done. When she was done whispering, she motioned "Shh" with her finger over her mouth because she hadn't told anyone yet. She shared how her boyfriend's a really good influence on her and hates that she works there. This caused her to work hard to find another job.

It was obvious from our conversation that whoever the ministry was that came into the establishment regularly really impacted her. I wish they could've experienced this encounter with me because the seeds they sowed were bearing fruit right in front of my eyes. They may never know until the other side of heaven how their consistency and love helped her exit this time of darkness in her life.

I laid my hand on her shoulder and whispered a quiet prayer over her so no one could overhear. I wasn't able to talk to any other girls because an elderly woman, who was their "madam," shushed us out the door and wouldn't let us interact for long with the girls. Each club has a woman in the dressing room who helps the girls "get ready," and who is designed to keep their spirits up.

Let's pray right now for this woman and her new job. We declare together that she'll never be sucked back into the strip club industry and that she'll have a new life in Christ Jesus.

Also say a prayer for the local outreach ministry. We pray they will continue to thrive and reach these women. Sometimes it can be so discouraging to come week after week and never see the fruit of your labor. We pray for their leader and all the volunteers to receive a fresh outpouring of God's love and anointing, and that they can reach into places no one else will go to be the hands and feet of Jesus. Lastly, pray for the madam and other madams who help to perpetuate the exploitation of their fellow sisters.

Bloody, Bruised, and Scarred

I had the honor to lead an overnight team in Minneapolis and was a little bit nervous at first. I attended the outreach the previous year in 2017 in Houston, Texas but the following year started differently. The atmosphere wasn't as heavy because I prepared my heart more this year. As a second year Chicago Master Commission student, I led a shift and was resolved to fight for the women who were lost and broken.

Our team began the evening going to strip clubs with a shift from 7 p.m. to 7 a.m. Most of the volunteers on my team had never conducted outreach in strip clubs and, in retrospect, that was probably where the heaviness stemmed.

Each club had people working at a front desk and the bouncers were friendly and inviting. Seeing all the faces of girls greatly disturbed me. Honestly, I wanted to save them all.

At one strip club we gained access to the girls' changing room. I was originally going toward a group of girls, however, I felt a nudge to go left instead. As soon as I turned left I noticed "Vanessa." She was a darker-skinned woman who had scars and bruises all over her body. They were so red and bloody and I couldn't help but tear up as I walked toward her.

I approached her with another volunteer as I tried to hold myself together. Initially she didn't look at us but eventually she made eye contact, as we continued a casual conversation. She wouldn't tell us where she was from, but based on her heavy accent and skin tone I suspected she was Brazilian.

We asked if she wanted prayer and all she could ask—more than once—was for us to pray for all the girls at the club and for the grace of God to be over their lives. She was so serious as she looked me in the eyes and repeated her request. My heart immediately got heavy and burdened for her and every other girl I'd encountered.

After every night of outreach I laid in bed with a deep desire to save and reach them all. As I tried to sleep I saw their faces and found it difficult to rest, knowing they were still suffering.

Pause and pray for Vanessa who wore her scars outwardly and inwardly.

Holy Spirit Prayer

I began a conversation with an extremely friendly woman who openly shared her life with our team. She spoke of her complete mistrust of men, which led her to marry a woman a few month prior to our encounter. They were trying to conceive a baby and asked me to pray for this request and her doctor's appointment she had in a few days. Believing homosexuality is not God's design for marriage, I couldn't pray that prayer.

We went to the bathroom and as I prayed, the Holy Spirit began to take over. My prayer didn't offend her, we loved her where she was at, and after we concluded, we all hugged. God knows all things and when I didn't know what to say, the Holy Spirit gave me words of truth and love.

Join us in praying for this woman who understandably has a complete mistrust of men, given all the trauma she has endured, and has turned to homosexuality. Also, pray for God to mend all those who have never encountered healthy relationships with men and don't know how to trust.

Pastor's Reflection

A group of women had just gained access into the strip club. A pastor who was volunteering on the trip waited outside to minister to the bouncers. During the debriefing that night the pastor said that when our volunteers opened the door to enter the strip club, he felt the presence of God so thick, just like it is on a Sunday when he preaches. As he was praying and the volunteers entered, he felt the Lord claim the club as Holy Ground.

Would you stop and pray for the strip clubs in your communities? Pray for God to use those going into them to minister, or if no outreach is taking place, to rise up ambassadors to reclaim ground the enemy has taken.

CHAPTER 4
AIRPORT OUTREACH

The football championship game is usually the first Sunday in February and as early as Wednesday, fans start arriving to begin celebrating their teams. With hundreds of thousands of fans flying into the host city, the airport becomes a busy place. We begin airport outreach Thursday by standing at baggage claim and TSA exits at each terminal during all hours of the day and night. We see women coming off the plane ready to "work." Some are alone and some are in packs, multiple girls with pimps. We often see some sitting and waiting for long periods of time for a ride to come pick them up.

During outreach, we give our standard takeaways to those we suspect are being trafficked, or those coming in specifically to work during the sporting event. We always err on the side of caution and if we provide something to a person who is just there celebrating as a fan, we explain part of our purpose is to raise awareness. We explain what takes place, give them our information, and ask them to report any suspicious activity they may see using the takeaway we give them.

It's always intriguing to train people in airport outreach with the main question being, "How will we know?" We provide training to recognize common signs. With several flights landing and girls waiting in baggage claim the volunteers are always appalled at how blatant and obvious it becomes to them. It's as if they had been traveling for years and suddenly a veil was removed from their eyes.

Often when we travel we are so focused on checking our bags, boarding our plane, getting off, reclaiming our luggage, and getting a ride to our eventual destination. When volunteers spend 12 straight hours in baggage claim specifically focusing on identifying victims, it's amazing how quickly they pick up on what's going on and vow they will never travel the same again because their eyes have been opened to a whole new world.

The following are a few interactions we've had during airport outreach.

Kid Decoy

I was sitting in the San Francisco airport baggage claim in 2016. We were a few hours into outreach and I saw a woman wearing promiscuous clothes. She had her head down and when she looked up she avoided eye contact. These (and many more) are all signs of trafficking. The airport was extremely packed because it was just a few days away from the big event when thousands of flights are arriving. I don't remember the statistics of how many planes landed each minute, but it was back-to-back-to-back. Our volunteers could barely keep up. The San Francisco harbor near the airport had planes visible in the air landing every minute.

I was mingling around baggage claim and saw something that really stood out. An older man came into the baggage claim area. He had three children with him who brought little plastic chairs. Now I have three small children at home, but these kids were beyond obedient. When they came into the baggage claim area, the man told them to put the chairs down and sit on them. They set them down, sat down, and were quiet as could be.

The man pulled out a phone and began texting. I stood just behind him and saw him type, "What are you wearing?" (Yes, I was snooping.) Then he picked up the phone and made a call. I saw the woman I had noticed exhibiting signs of being trafficked answer one of two phones in her hand. Having two phones was common, with one being a personal phone and another to receive calls from clients. She and the man were having a discussion about where to meet. From the conversation it was apparent this was the first time they were meeting each other.

The woman was waiting for her baggage to arrive and the man with the three children sitting on chairs was a little ways away, watching and waiting. I decided to casually approach the woman at the baggage claim as if I was waiting for luggage. She was looking down at her phone and was very standoffish. Polite but meek. I gave her a rose and told her if she wasn't safe she could pull the card off the rose and throw the rose away. I let her know there was help if she contacted the number located on the card. She accepted the rose and said, "Thank you," all while not making a lot of eye contact but instead sheepishly looking down.

I kept pacing around the baggage claim as if waiting for the buzzer to sound to get my baggage. The man was watching me. Once the woman got her bags, she made her way over to him. I was standing within a few feet. He called out to the kids, "Look kids, Mommy is home." She smiled and the kids picked up their chairs, barely acknowledged the woman as she said hello, and they were on their way.

As I said, I have children and when I get off the plane after being away from them, they practically tackle me in pure excitement. It was obvious these were not this woman's children. In addition, while they were standing in the same baggage claim section for 15 to 20 minutes waiting for the baggage to arrive, this man never approached her with the children when they were in eyeshot range. It wasn't until he noticed me and saw me approach her that he used the kids as a decoy.

My heart sank but I was grateful she got a rose and business card with our information on it if she needed help. Join us in praying for the woman and the children who I truly believe were used as a decoy. Who knows what environment they're in. Don't forget to also pray for the older man who isn't out of God's reach. In Jesus' name.

Pimps and Trafficked on Our Plane

2015, we're leaving Chicago and on our way to Phoenix, Arizona, to minister and rescue those trafficked at the big national football game there. I'm debriefing the team at the gate, and suddenly we realized there were pimps all around us, their women spread out sitting in different places. We stopped our discussion. Men were casually checking in on different girls sitting throughout the waiting area, and through observations before, during and after our flight, we counted 14 girls and 6 pimps on our plane going to the venue where the championship game was taking place.

After seeing all I have, it infuriates me to read articles that report trafficking doesn't increase during the football championship game;

claiming it's only a myth. Ours was just one plane full of pimps and trafficking victims, and thousands of airplanes were seen arriving the week of the game with the similar make up. Every year on every flight, both coming to and leaving the venue, I have personally seen pimps and those being trafficked on my flight.

The women on our flight in 2015 were dressed extremely provocatively, appearing ready to start work the moment they stepped off the plane. As soon as we boarded our flight it was loud and filled with partying. People were drinking, chanting their team's name, and rivalry was already in the air. We saw the pimps periodically checking on the different women spread out on the plane, and when they exited, the women walked ahead towards the baggage claim, separate from each other. Once they got to the carousel, the pimp got the bags and they all quickly left together.

One Caucasian male was no younger than 60, and when we got off the plane, he literally had a strong clutch on the arm of an African-American girl who appeared younger than 20 years old. She looked scared and avoided any kind of eye contact. He had her under such close watch that we couldn't give her any information. My heart wrenched.

Another very young-looking girl on our plane had no luggage and instead boarded the plane with a garbage bag filled with all her essentials for the few days she would be there. Her clothes were tattered. She looked Middle Eastern and also avoided any eye contact. Through our hours of observations before during and after our flight, we discerned she wasn't being pimped and was by herself.

When we got off the airplane some of our team members approached her and asked if we could help. She said she was okay, but she did let them pray for her. We walked together to the baggage claim but she never claimed a bag. She had all her belongings in the trash bag she carried over her shoulder. Our team members took turns and helped carry the heavy trash bag.

Once we arrived at baggage claim she sat down on a bench and we decided to wait to make sure she was okay. While we walked together to baggage claim, I observed her with two telephones, presumably one personal phone and one for escort calls.

We observed for at least 45 minutes and she was still in baggage claim, waiting, glued to her phone. We approached her several times and asked if she wanted to come with us because we had a shelter for those we rescued in Phoenix where they found permanent placements.

We learned she worked at strip clubs in Chicago, and was coming to work at clubs in Phoenix the week of the game to make money. When she realized no one was going to pick her up, she agreed to let us take her to an Airbnb where she was staying for the week.

In 2018, flying from Memphis, Tennessee, to Minneapolis, Minnesota, I again saw pimps and girls on the planes I flew to and from the venue. On the way home I noticed a few girls who didn't appear to be with anyone who was pimping them but who were dressed extremely provocatively.

Please stop and pray for all these girls and pimps we encountered on our planes and for airline personnel to recognize the signs, not to be deceived, and to report suspicious activity to the authorities.

Airline Assistance

San Francisco, California, 2016. I passed out roses with our business card attached for hours at the airport. A few days later, we got a call from a woman who said she received a rose with our information on it at the airport and she needed help. When she got to San Francisco she was scheduled to stay at an Airbnb with a group of people but said she got "kicked out."

The woman attempted to change her ticket because she wasn't scheduled to leave until three days later after the championship game. However, when she called the airline, they wanted $500 to change her travel itinerary—$500 she didn't have, and so she was stranded with nowhere to stay. That's when she remembered the rose and card she received at the airport.

We quickly contacted the airline and explained how we help those who were trafficked during the week of the game. Through countless calls and being transferred too many times to recall, our fearless volunteer was able to get the ticket changed and the fee waived.

Our volunteers picked her up, fragile and scared, and brought her to the airport where she was able to go home early. We stayed in touch with her for a few weeks after we left the game to make sure she was okay. During one of her texts after the game, I felt she needed help by going into a residential program but she wasn't ready.

Stop and say a prayer for this young woman who placed herself in a very vulnerable situation, BUT GOD graced her to get home safely.

We are grateful for the airline that waived the fee and we pray for continued protection around her. We planted a seed...Lord, send someone to water it, in Jesus' name.

Early Morning Arrival

We were at the airport on Thursday at 5 a.m. to intercept flights arriving with human trafficking victims the week of the game taking place on Sunday. I saw a woman at baggage claim whom I follow on social media. She operates a safe house in Las Vegas for trafficking survivors and is often asked to speak on the issue.

I learned earlier in the month she was speaking on a panel the week of the sporting event on the subject. I approached her and introduced myself, trying not to sound like a groupie. She asked me, "Are you doing outreach right now? There's a pimp [pointing bluntly] and his two girls right there who were all on my plane."

We'd also spotted them and were trying to get an opportune time to slip the women a pack of tissue with contact information for help. The pimp turned around with their luggage on a cart and began to push it with the women walking right behind him. I was able to slip each of them the tissue and whisper softly, "There's information on there if you need anything." They smiled politely, nodded their heads, and kept walking behind their pimp. They were dressed ready to work, and our hearts sank.

Stop and pray for these two young women and this pimp who were coming from a major metropolis, Las Vegas, known for trafficking women in strip clubs, casinos, and major hotel chains. Also, stop and pray for the Christ-based organization that the woman we encountered in baggage claim founded and operates. God knows their specific needs and the needs of their leader who is a national ambassador on the issue of human trafficking in America.

CHAPTER 5
HOTEL AND BROTHEL OUTREACH

Under and Outside the Door

We were staying in a hotel in Oakland, California, 2016, and got word from one of our partner organizations that trafficking was taking place in their hotel, which was within walking distance from ours. A few of us walked down with our outreach supplies—roses and business cards with our contact information—to see if we could intercept any victims.

As we arrived, we saw a large group of girls with a man in the parking lot, and we pretended to be waiting for someone while we tried to listen to their conversation. It became more and more apparent that something wasn't right, based on all their body language.

We followed at a distance. When they got on the elevator, we acted as if we were going to our room on the same floor and casually engaged in small talk. In reality, we were following them to see what room they went into.

As we approached, the door to their room opened and we saw liquor bottles and more girls in the room before they closed the door. We kept walking and went around the corner to pray about what we should do. The men left and went to the elevator and at that point we decided to go to the room, shove a bunch of business cards under the door with our information, and leave four roses outside the door. Afterwards we reported what we witnessed to hotel management.

We prayed the men didn't intercept the information and that the girls in the room found their way to freedom. Let's intercede for these precious daughters of the Most High! We took a picture that's posted on the Skyway Railroad social media Instagram and Facebook on February 28, 2016, if you're interested in liking and following all God does through this ministry.

Room 109

We'd broken into our outreach teams for the evening and were in our hotel lobby located across the street from the Mall of America. I was going over expectations and what we would be doing. After praying, a group of people went to the area where our outreach supplies were being stored so they could fill up backpacks.

All of a sudden I saw a girl walk in the hotel front door by herself. She was wearing high-heel boots above her knees, and if there was something above it I couldn't see because her coat was longer than any shirt, dress, or shorts. I motioned to another volunteer and we bolted down the hall after her.

About 30 paces behind her was her pimp who was going to wait in the hotel lobby. We finally caught up with the woman and were able to give her our contact information. We saw the room she was about to go into—room 109 in this hotel. (I guarantee every reader has stayed in this national hotel chain at one time in their life.)

One of our men came and stood at the end of the hallway in between us and the pimp in the lobby because the pimp saw us run after her. Within two minutes the girl came out of the room, and as she was approaching her pimp yells, "What the f***?"

We believe he saw us go after her, thought it was a bust, so he texted or called her to abort without her knowing why. That's why she came back extremely frustrated. Room 109 didn't get this girl whom we intercepted ever so briefly. Unfortunately, other volunteers later saw another girl come in through the lobby and go to that same room.

We designed business cards for johns with information to lead the man to what they believed was an online escorting website. However, when they went to the site and clicked on one of the pictures of a girl, they were redirected to XXX church's website and presented the gospel of Jesus Christ. There was also a sex addiction assessment on the link.

When we got back to the hotel after conducting outreach, I went with another volunteer to room 109 and a "Do Not Disturb" sign was hooked on the doorknob. Unfortunately, we knew what that meant and when I see one in the future I'll always think of this encounter. I took about 20 of these cards for johns and shoved them under the door of room 109.

Pause and pray for him, the two girls who went to his room, and the pimp.

Uniformed Disgrace

We were on a block in San Francisco known as the Tenderloin District. We spent literally one hour parked on this block, heavy with drug activity and prostitution. While we were parked, we saw a massage parlor (brothel) and observed men going in and out the entire time we were there.

Men would ring the doorbell and someone would open the metal gate door through which we could see stairs leading down. Men entered and were gone for about 30 minutes and then come back out. After witnessing this, I next saw something that both sickened and saddened my heart. A police officer, dressed in his uniform, went to the door, rang the bell, went inside for 30 minutes, and then left.

Stop and take a moment to pray for this officer, that he find the light amidst his hypocrisy, and for the girls he chose to exploit rather than protect. He needs God's love to help turn away from the darkness that lead him to ring that doorbell.

Mockery on the Streets

San Francisco, 2016. We were in the same Tenderloin District at the same brothel that we learned is an Asian massage parlor. It's the one we saw a uniformed police officer enter the day before.

We rang the bell, and a person who was living on the streets and sitting right next to the door pointed at us and laughed in a mocking tone: "Ahhh, you are going to that place?" He spoke as if everyone knew what was going on inside. He thought it was hilarious that we were going in as customers.

A woman, who looked to be in her 60s and must have been the madam, came to the door. Behind the gated door were stairs leading to a business in the basement. The madam could barely walk down the stairs but invited us to go in. Gaining access was extremely rare because most Asian massage parlors are very private and the madams won't even answer the door if they see a group of women through the security camera (which they all have) pointed at the door. We often have male volunteers ring the bell as a decoy, and when they buzz the door, all the women come from behind and go through the doors.

Once we got downstairs, we saw an open area with couches in what appeared to be a waiting area. Doors led to private rooms on one wall that went all the way down a hallway.

We saw four girls—three Asian and one young Caucasian girl who was dressed in sweatpants, a T-shirt, and slippers, with her hair messy on top of her head. By the way she was dressed, it looked like she lived there but was not on shift. We gave her a bag and her demeanor was very hard with little to no eye contact. The girls were called from behind doors and down the hall and we were told to stay in the waiting area while girls came to us to receive a bag.

We gave gifts to each of the girls and then left. Walking back up those stairs I felt my heart breaking. They all had fake smiles and kept repeating, "Thank you, thank you, thank you." But we left them in darkness. I can still see the white couches in the dimly lit waiting area with fake flowers as decor and a woman behind a counter where customers would pay. These images will never leave me.

Please stop and say a prayer for this madam and all the girls and customers we encountered in that basement brothel. It was a mockery on the streets, including the police officer who took an oath of office to uphold the law and protect citizens. Pray for corruption to be uprooted and darkness to be exposed.

Collusion with Hotel Management

Oakland, California, 2016. Our team arrived in Oakland, outside of San Francisco, on the Saturday before the big event. The first part of the week was spent going to all the venues we had mapped out prior to the game, making sure they were open and creating routes for safe escape. We also had teams of volunteers who prepared the outreach supplies. Over 500 live roses were delivered to the hotel and we de-thorned them and tied our business cards around them. We also filled gift bags with items we gave to women at strip clubs.

The weather was beautiful and a huge deck outside the hotel protruded into the bay. Early in the week, we began sitting there and getting all our supplies ready. We were staying at a lower end motel because the rates for rooms the week of the game are extremely expensive and we were staying 10 nights.

When we checked in I had a long conversation with the motel lobby clerk and explained what we were doing there. He indicated that their team received training on human trafficking and how to identify it in preparation for the game. This pleased me and I informed him if he saw anything, to give those who were being trafficked our business cards. He also allowed us to leave them on the check-in counter for the week.

On Tuesday we began noticing a group of very young beautiful Asian girls who arrived with men. A few of our team approached the girls and gave them a business card, the men watching us at every move. We began to get our supplies ready inside our motel room and not outside so we would be out of their sight.

As the week went on, it became increasingly apparent that this group was operating a trafficking ring. More and more girls arrived and we saw them get out of a nice car and pop the trunk filled with liquor bottles. The girls—dressed in high heel pumps, short skirts, and low-cut shirts—all grabbed drinks. Although it was only mid-morning, they were already intoxicated and laughing profusely to fit in with the rest of the girls. They looked so young.

By Wednesday the number and races of the girls with them increased. At one point I opened my door and was shocked to see them on the pier with a white sheet from the hotel room hanging from the pergola as a backdrop. The girls were completely naked and the men were taking pictures and videos of them. We know they were getting the footage necessary to post ads on backpage and other sites right in front of our eyes. One of our volunteers even saw a film crew come in and observed them taping a pornographic movie in one of the rooms.

I was infuriated. It was so blatant and in our face, as if Satan himself was mocking us. I was ready to march over to the motel lobby, but then I witnessed something that made me want to throw up. One of the motel management was standing with one of the pimps laughing and I saw the pimp slip him money, and then the motel clerk went back to the lobby. Great! So the motel was in on this as well and took money to keep quiet.

I called two federal law enforcement agencies but nothing happened. By Friday I couldn't take it anymore; it was obviously going on all around us. We saw the girls bringing johns up the stairs to a room above us and the pimp watching from outside his room within steps of ours. All night, up and down, with him standing outside his room where the videotaping was going on earlier in the week.

I decided to call local police and inform them what was going on. I rounded up about 10 prayer warriors in a room and we began to wage war. What happened in the motel room was the most profound encounter I've experienced with the Lord. For a detailed account, read the next testimony titled: "A Visit from the Archangel Michael."

Before proceeding, though, please pause and pray for every girl we encountered in the trafficking ring at our hotel, the pimps, and the motel management...specifically pray that management will be part of the solution and not contribute to the atrocities taking place inside every hotel chain, the upscale and low-end.

A Visit from the Archangel Michael

A huge trafficking ring was operating in the low-end hotel where our team was staying in Oakland, California, 2016. We tried bringing in federal and local authorities but they did not respond. So instead we gathered a group of prayer warriors and went into one of our rooms to pray them out of our midst and to protect the women.

That day we all saw and witnessed different things. Heaven will only tell what the women, girls, and men encountered that night who were the recipients of our warfare. One woman on the team, Deanna, was a minister with a special anointing. She's since gone to be with the Lord, but my profound encounter with her that day will always be central to my heart because the call of God on my life was revealed in those moments.

She was going around the room praying for each person on the team and each woman visibly encountered Jesus at a higher level. She approached me last and when she came to me, she stopped right in from of me with her arms outstretched. We both fell to our knees face-to-face, and then we fell flat on the floor with our cheeks pressed together. Someone captured a picture memorializing that encounter, for which I'm eternally grateful.

When we fell to the ground, I felt a heaviness and weight on my back, suffocating the air out of me. I could barely breathe and the heaviness of the darkness all around me was overpowering. I felt like

I was falling, spiraling into a huge black hole and there was torment all around me. In retrospect it reminded me of "gnashing of teeth" that's described in the Bible (Matthew 13:42 NIV, Luke 13:28 NIV).

I was trying to say the name of "Jesus" and "Bring the light. It's so dark. Bring the light." My voice was a faint whisper coming out of my mouth because of the immense pressure on my back. The weight of agony all around me was too much to bear. I was screaming but only whimpers and gasps were coming out. As my spirit cried out to the deep for "the light," I started seeing shimmering flickers of light in front and on the sides of my eyes. The weight was subsiding and the agony was dissipating.

After the prayer was over I asked each person to share what they experienced. I knew all our encounters were interconnected and we each saw a different piece of the puzzle. One woman in the room said the minister who prayed over me asked for protection at the beginning of the week when they first arrived and for angels to protect us all week...and not just any angels, but she commanded the Archangel Michael to go before us the week of outreach and protect us.

The woman described seeing the Archangel Michael in the room when the woman came to pray for me. She described him as being huge and towering over the whole room with his wings spread out over us. She said he came over to me and put his hands on my hips and that's when I fell to my knees and on my face. She also said he was on top of me, which explains all the pressure I felt.

I firmly believe the Archangel Michael brought me that day to the pit of hell, allowing me to encounter the torture and pain of the women I'm called to reach. I've never experienced something so dark and oppressive. It's like I felt where they were and what they went through.

As I kept calling on the name of Jesus and for the light, I believe the angel began lifting me back up and this was the flicking of light I saw—his wings. I knew from that moment I was marked for God's purpose to reach, rescue, and speak life into those bound in human trafficking.

Now before you write this off as being too charismatic, as a lawyer I'm the most unlikely suspect. I'm logical Lucy. Yet this was such a profound, real encounter. It's hard to even put in words the magnitude of what I experienced because His encounters are indescribable.

I'm overwhelmingly grateful and my life will never be the same. I have no idea why God chose me (maybe because I am logical Lucy), but He did. And I will daily pick up my cross and fulfill the assignment He showed me that day in Oakland, California, in the middle of a huge underage trafficking ring at a corrupted motel.

I don't know how long we were in the room praying. All I know is when we were done and walked out, there wasn't one pimp or one girl left in the motel, to the glory of God. We declared it Holy Ground and we never saw them again. It was a lesson that we can call on man to come break up evil schemes, but even better we can call upon the name of the Lord and His light will always outshine the darkness.

Would you stop right now and say a prayer for the family and children of Minister Deanna who God used tremendously that night and who abruptly went to be with the Lord. We all miss her dearly and we celebrate the legacy she planted in each of us. She has children so please say a prayer for them and all those we encountered the night of this powerful prayer.

Petrified John

We stopped at a brothel in 2016 in San Francisco that was located on a corner lot. It was after midnight and the place wasn't in a busy area at all. We walked in and there was a woman behind the counter who spoke very little English. She appeared to be a middle-aged Russian woman.

While we were telling her we had gifts for the women, a man walked in who was in his late 20s to early 30s. He was extremely edgy and nervous and looked all around him to see if anyone was watching.

When he came in, the woman told him what the price was and he was insistent about not wanting to pay with a credit card but with cash, repeating it over and over. I've never witnessed someone so anxious and on edge...fidgeting, clumsy, talking fast with broken sentences as he paced and kept looking side to side to see who was there. Our presence definitely made him uncomfortable.

It was apparent the woman wasn't going to let us give the bags to the girls, but I decided to linger until after the man was escorted to a room. The woman quickly swished him back to a room and when she returned she told us, "No, thank you."

I am married and enjoy getting massages, especially on vacation. However, I cannot imagine booking a massage for my husband or myself in a brothel where girls are actually performing sexual acts for their customers. In the "Johns Boards" where men discuss which massage parlors are brothels, they often talk about which ones have "HE," their code word for happy endings.

My eyes were completely opened and I'll never look at massage parlors open late at night the same ever again. Even though we didn't get to see any of the girls in that brothel, I got to witness the torment a john feels as he feeds an addiction that has him bound in secrecy and not wanting to leave a trace with a credit card transaction. Who knows if he had a wife or children at home?

Please pause and pray for the women at that corner brothel, the Russian madam, and the anxious man.

My Own Backyard

The world is far from perfect which we all know. Each one of us deals with the stresses, problems, and evils we see in the world a little differently. Some people choose to face them head-on, while others seek to hide as if they could somehow avoid them altogether. Yet, there's one specific evil (human trafficking) many people have encountered, perhaps unknowingly, and still insist "it simply doesn't happen" or "it doesn't happen here...maybe somewhere else." I find it hard to believe people claim this atrocity doesn't exist. It not only exists in our own lifetime but surprisingly it exists in our own communities—in your own community. The evil of human trafficking is a modern-day slavery, and it's very real.

In 2018 I had the opportunity to serve on a team of more than 40 volunteers during one of America's largest sporting events, which just so happened to take place in my home state of Minnesota. This sporting event is famous for bringing all sorts of fans, players, celebrities, and broadcasters from all over the United States—and sadly, is also notorious for bringing the biggest influx of human trafficking Minnesota was probably ever going to see.

The team and I had the opportunity to lead various outreaches to promote prevention and awareness and also made attempts to reach and rescue those trapped in the horrors of human trafficking. After this life-changing week of outreach and rescue, I can say with certainty that there's a difference between believing something exists and experiencing it personally.

One particular outreach took place in the lobby bar of a very high-end chain of hotels. You'd certainly be familiar with this hotel chain and have undoubtedly even stayed there before .

We went into the lobby in two separate groups—one all women and the other all men. We spent hours in the hotel bar in hopes of spotting possible victims of human trafficking. Some of the men would have conversations with women. During the conversations, they'd slip them a business card with information on how to get resources to help them get out of dangerous situations and even be rescued by our team who were there all week.

The ladies in our group were there to help keep eyes on the men to make sure there were no immediate dangers. They also tried to talk with the ladies to give them information on how to escape. During our time at this hotel bar, there were many women working that night. While it was easy to tell who they were, it was difficult to make actual contact with them.

After spending numerous hours in the hotel bar I saw a glimpse into a world I knew existed, but never truly understood and witnessed. I saw woman after woman bringing "men" up to their hotel rooms, only to return later to the bar and start the process over. I use quotes to describe these "men" because a real man (or john, as they are referred to) doesn't buy sex.

What broke my heart the most was seeing the looks on the women's faces before they saw their next "client." I looked into the eyes of one young lady, and I saw nothing behind them except for pain and desperation—emptiness. I've never seen such sadness in another human's eyes. As she looked past me to a man at the bar, her face changed. It was as if she was putting on a mask and turning on a neon "open" sign as she smiled at him. Her expression changed, but her eyes did not.

Throughout the course of the evening I observed what was clearly a madam (essentially a lady pimp) and a pimp arranging for these women to be sold all night in the hotel bar. At one point, the madam approached our group of women and made hand motions, signaling she was watching us. I also noticed people on the next floor taking pictures of us with a professional camera. It was obvious they were keeping a very close eye on us. They knew very quickly why we were there and didn't like it.

The encounters I experienced opened my eyes here in my own state like never before. I saw evil like I've never seen. The activity I witnessed was a little more than an hour's drive from where I live and there was a ring of human trafficking happening right in front of me.

One of the women in our group asked one of the waitresses at the bar if she'd seen any prostitution happening that night and she said she hadn't. Yet, it was blatant and obviously happening constantly all that night right in front of her face. Sadly, everyone turned a blind eye.

After what I saw and experienced in the hotel bar, I can no longer bury my head in the sand and simply wish for it to go away. We must all, as mankind, stand and be the voices for the voiceless. Our team can never again act as though we haven't understood the evil that's made itself present in our time and hope by our inaction good may prevail.

This evil exists during our time and it's our responsibility to decide what we'll do with the time God's given to us. We should all, however painful the process, have a moment like our team had in that hotel bar.

My hope is that through reading this, you have an encounter and I pray it hits close to home, where your eyes can be opened, your heart can become broken, and your mouth can speak against this horrible injustice. Let's not do nothing, be nothing, or say nothing. Instead, let's together become a voice from outside the stadium for those who cannot speak.

Pause and pray for these girls at the hotel bar, the "men" who paid for their services, the men and women who were exploiting them, and for the hotel industry to courageously report human trafficking when they see it.

CHAPTER 6
STREET OUTREACH

While a lot of prostitution and human trafficking takes place on the streets, it's sometimes difficult to find the "tracks" (streets and areas known for trafficking) because we're not from the venue when we minister the week of the sporting events. We have a trained volunteer who conducts hours of online research on "Johns Boards" where men talk about their encounters and where to go for sexual acts. We also coordinate with local ministries familiar with the area who conduct outreach, if any exist.

However, because most of the prostitution taking place on the streets are those being trafficked locally and our mission is to reach, rescue, and place those being flown in and trafficked for the game, we don't spend as much time on street outreach as we do in the other venues.

Many we encounter being trafficked on the street have drug problems and often need detox before we can place them. We've found nationally there's a shortage of detox beds available, especially at all hours of the night for those with no insurance or identification.

The following are a few of the encounters during our street intervention at the annual sporting event outreach.

Relentless Pursuit 500 Miles From Home

Minneapolis, Minnesota, February 2018. We were doing street outreach in an area known for human trafficking. The first woman I felt prompted to engage with was a middle-aged woman dressed in a red jumpsuit. I followed her as she crossed the parking lot into a liquor store. "Followed" is a loose term. "Darted for her" is a better expression. I finally caught up with her inside the overly-lit store where she picked up a liquor bottle off the top shelf.

As I headed towards her, she stared at me as if I invaded the unspoken appropriate social bubble in these kinds of establishments. "Hi, I am ..... I am with....," I blurted out and a strange look followed. I could see every wall of protection she'd built through years of life. Another volunteer on our team came inside just as we began our exchange and asked the woman, "Where are you from?" She casually responded, "Omaha." My heart immediately leaped. This was no "casual" response and certainly was not a "casual" encounter!

"So what?" you may ask. Here I was 500 miles away from my home, Omaha, and the first person I'm ministering to is also from Omaha. God has a great sense of humor. She was with another woman who came behind her mid-conversation.

Our encounter didn't end there. We prayed for her, and because we're from the same city I invited her to my home church. As soon as I mentioned the name of my church, she said she knew someone who attended there. Turns out the very person she knew was my best friend with whom I do human trafficking outreach ministry!

You cannot make this stuff up. We don't serve a "casual" God. We serve a supernatural God who will pursue us to all ends of the Earth, just like He did for these Omaha women in Minneapolis at a liquor store!

To put this improbable encounter in perspective, more than 70,000 people traveled to be inside the stadium cheering for their team, countless others came to the venue and didn't even attend the event, thousands of individuals are flown in and trafficked the week of the event, and a reported 18 organizations (and all their volunteers) participated in outreach that week in Minnesota.

Yet, at that specific time and at that specific liquor store, these two women (who drove all the way to the event to "work") encountered one of our many volunteers with one being from her same city, all while she was picking up a bottle of "spirits." Little did she know the Lord was giving her His Spirit instead. The improbability and impossibility of this encounter show God's relentless love and pursuit for the one out of the 99.

Would you stop right now and pray for these two women for

whom God turned a casual encounter into a divine blessing? We pray for His continued relentless pursuit of them even right now and that we'd encounter them again, this time 500 miles back in Omaha, Nebraska.

Oppressed Eyes

One of my hardest yet most precious moments was on Hennepin Avenue in Minneapolis, Minnesota, 2018. We'd just crossed the street from a club reaching out to girls entering to "work." I noticed a man with two girls at his side walking down the street toward the north end. One of the women kept looking down, cowering, and made no eye contact. He kept her close.

I bumped alongside one of the girls and tucked a pack of the tissues–which had an outreach number on it–under her right arm. She held it tightly. The man broke focus during a brief moment. I looked ahead as they walked down the street. Then it was as if someone saw me...they saw me and knew.

I could do nothing else but pray protection and freedom for her. Such a brief encounter, but one marked with the reality of these two girls' circumstances and so many others.

Stop and pray right now that these two beautiful gems, who God knows by name, would find freedom where they can hold their heads up confidently, with the ability to look people in the eyes again because they know who they are in Christ Jesus. We also pray for this man who was controlling these two women, that God would impress upon him the true identity of being a man...and not just any man, but a man after God's own heart.

Homeless Youth with a Destiny

Saturday night, we took Minneapolis' light rail train into the downtown area where all the partying would take place. I've always prayed for eyes to see the pain of others, which manifested during our train ride. A young man sat across from me. I kept looking at him and finally, we made eye contact, smiling. I sparked up a conversation and he said he was "21." I understood that was a common answer with street kids.

He spoke of being estranged from his parents and noted he was part of a homeless youth program. I began to speak truths into his life and the destiny he was born for. He allowed me to pray for him.

When he left, he wore an awesome glow and a smile again on his face. I believe it was a moment in his path. Join our team in praying for every seed planted on the train into this young homeless man and other homeless youth. We pray the seed continues to be watered by the Lord for his great destiny to be fulfilled, in Jesus' name.

Party Bus

Minneapolis, Minnesota, February 2018. It was so incredibly cold. My hands and face felt frostbitten from being outside for even short amounts of time. We took a break and went inside a building that looked like an indoor mall downtown, right off Nichollete Mall where the main event festivities were taking place.

As we were standing there trying to warm up before braving the cold again, we saw a group of at least 15 to 20 women of all ethnic backgrounds with very little clothing on, along with two men. We tried to engage the women and give them tissue but none of them were interested. They politely brushed us off, saying, "No, thank you."

They were all standing by the door looking outside as if they were waiting for someone. Very loud, they appeared to be having a grand ol' time. My heart was so broken. We believe they were waiting for a party bus to pick them up and the two men were the ones "in charge" for the evening. Strip clubs around the U.S. take girls over state lines to events at other clubs or places they have set up. We believe these girls all knew each other and were taken from somewhere to provide entertainment outside their "regular" venue.

Girls are brought to dance in party buses that in essence are mobile strip clubs equipped with poles and areas for the male "visitors." One of the volunteers on our team commented how the two men with all the girls were both extremely short with all the women towering over them. Their stature didn't suggest power, but that was obviously not the case.

Even though these women weren't interested in speaking to any of us or receiving the tissue packets with contact information, let's stop and pray for them. God knows each of their names and the men who were escorting them to wherever they were going.

More Than Just a Cut and Shave

We were conducting street outreach in Minneapolis at around 11:00 p.m. on Lake Street, which is known for prostitution. Although we came in from out of town and weren't familiar with where the tracks were located, our trained volunteers had already done their research on "Johns Boards." Thus, we knew from the john's own posts that Lake Street was where we'd find those being trafficked.

We drove up and down Lake Street that first night, from 1st Street through around 35th Street. Because of the cold, we didn't see many girls standing outside, which the johns complained about online.

We drove by a building with glass front windows stretching from the ground to the ceiling. The windows were completely filled with condensation from the warmth coming from the inside compared to the below zero freezing cold on the outside. It was one of those places where you could literally feel the heaviness and the darkness around and in the building. There was a weight over my spirit when we drove by.

We circled back around after passing it the first time because we saw a girl come out of the door and jump into a car that had pulled up. As we continued to watch, we saw this take place several times and quickly realized there were girls "working" and the place was a barbershop. We decided to walk by it and look inside so we could casually assess safety.

It was difficult to see inside because of all the condensation, but it looked as if it was all men inside sitting in barber chairs. We, therefore, felt it wasn't safe for us to go inside. When we drove by multiple times, there were definitely women coming out to get in customers' cars. As time passed, we also noticed several men standing outside the entrance, as though watching for activity to beckon a girl when a customer pulled up.

The last time we drove by the shop, we prayed the place down and declared it Holy Ground and a sanctuary. When we came back about an hour later, it was closed down with all the lights off. Hallelujah!

We don't know who owns that barbershop, but let's pray the police shut it down. Several times we saw police on Segways patrolling up and down Lake Street, so we know they're aware of what is going on inside. Let's pray that the darkness in and around that establishment be revealed and permanently shut down. Also lift up every girl and man inside the establishment and every customer who pulled up that night...that God would show His saving grace to each of them.

Did you stop and pray? Remember, we encourage you to not quickly breeze through these encounters, but instead engage in the girls' healing and freedom by invading heaven with your prayers.

No Habla Español

The first night we walked on Lake Street in Minneapolis, we encountered three people in a row who spoke only Spanish. Not anticipating this, we didn't have any bilingual volunteers with us. I could speak very broken Spanish and we were able to pray for one woman who was in the United States but her entire family was in Mexico. We couldn't understand each other but when we started praying for her in English, she began crying despite the language barrier. While we may not speak the same earthly language, God allowed us to speak to her through our heavenly language of prayer and we know God heard her prayers that night.

After around 45 minutes of street outreach, we decided that we needed to go back to our hotel about 30 minutes away and get one of the team members who spoke Spanish. Before leaving, we prayed up and down Lake Street and claimed each place we saw prostitution coming in and out of as "Holy Ground" and "God's Sanctuary."

When we came back about an hour later with a Spanish speaker, the place was COMPLETELY empty! Hallelujah! It truly became Holy Ground!

Please pause and pray for those working the streets who are immigrants and often work to send money back to family and children in their home country.

From Rejection, to Arrogance, to Deliverance

Doing outreach in 2016 in San Francisco will stay with me for the rest of my life. On one particular night I was with a team with two young ladies and a young man from Chicago Masters Commission. We were walking the streets during the week of the major sporting event and must've walked seven blocks looking for girls who were being trafficked. However, there were no girls in sight. We noticed prostitution going on in the San Francisco hotel lobbies earlier that week, so we decided to change our location and go there.

In one hotel we saw three beautiful girls with long pitch black hair leaving the lobby. We handed the first woman we approached one of the roses with our business card as a symbol of the love of Christ, letting her know she wasn't forgotten and was special. She said she was "allergic to roses," declined the flower, and walked away.

The second girl we encountered was very arrogant and laughed at us. One of the Master's Commission students asked her if we could pray for her. She said, "Yes! I want a man!"

What happened next was a miracle. The student began to pray saying, "Heavenly Father, I pray You'd send this woman a man who's worthy of her love. May he honor and respect her and be a blessing in her life."

The girl was shocked! Through the powerful prayer, she became very humbled, with tears in her eyes. Suddenly the trafficked woman said to God in the middle of our prayer, "Please help my cousin. She needs prayer!" So not only did this woman (who earlier greeted us with a hardened heart and arrogant attitude) receive prayer, so did her cousin.

The third and final girl we encountered was in her early 20s, very thin, frail, and sickly looking. "Gigi" could barely stand and appeared to be on drugs. I was filled with concern when I looked at her. I knew she was the reason we walked those seven blocks to speak into her life. I started to pray for her and noticed an evil eye on her necklace that I covered with my hand. As I prayed she cried out, "Help me! Help me!"

I knew she was demon-possessed. I instructed her to say the name of "Jesus!" Looking straight into her eyes I said, "Say Jesus again!" She mumbled but couldn't say His name. As I looked into her eyes I literally saw demons looking at me. I became louder and authoritative in my prayer, claiming healing upon her body.

She spoke of having pain all over her body that she described as rheumatoid arthritis. The two Master's Commission students touched her hands and feet as I prayed for her and we all claimed healing.

I asked her, "Do you believe Jesus can heal you?" and she responded affirmatively. With that answer and her faith rising, I said, "Okay, we declare in the mighty name of Jesus, be healed! And once you receive your miracle, promise you will seek God and look for a church where the Holy Spirit lives and serve Him for the rest of your life. Expect a miracle!"

She proceeded to repeat after us the "our Father who art in heaven prayer," then began crying out, "Nobody loves me."

I cried with her and said, "Jesus loves you. I love you! Who comes from Chicago to look for you on these dark streets in hopes that you would want a new beginning?! Me! God sent you His angels. Now believe! I love you!"

We all cried together, and she said she'd call the number on the card the following day. Everyone hugged and we left. This encounter was life-changing for all of us.

Thank You, Lord, for allowing me to be a part of Your miracle. Pause and pray for these women, for complete healing and deliverance.

Drug Addiction

Minneapolis, Minnesota, 2018. During my shift I went out to do street outreach in areas known as hot spots for human trafficking. Because we went out early, we didn't see a lot of activity so we went back to our hotel room where I helped prepare more awareness items.

Going out later at around 12:30 a.m. we encountered many girls, most of whom had signs of being heavily on drugs, some barely being able to walk. We met one girl named "Red" who at first wanted to come with us. However, she quickly became paranoid and walked off saying she "needed to get to the projects" and said someone was looking for her.

After that encounter, we gave a few more roses with business cards on them to women. The next day I got to participate in helping with two rescues which were very rewarding and eye-opening. I also worked in the call center and placed awareness items in bathrooms at truck stops in and around Minneapolis.

Please pray for Red and the other girls we encountered that evening who had strongholds of addiction. Pray for barriers to access detox facilities to be minimized throughout our country so those who really want permanent healing can receive it when outreach ministries rescue them at all hours of the day and night.

CHAPTER 7
ONLINE OUTREACH

A lot of trafficking takes place online through websites like backpage.com. (Sidebar: on 4/6/18 the FBI and other federal agencies seized this website. The two founders and other employees were indicted on 93 counts of criminal activity. In addition, their CEO (who at the time of publication was cooperating with authorities) pled guilty in three states to money laundering and human trafficking. These are huge victories in curbing online human trafficking.)

We have specially trained volunteers who find ads and extrapolate demographic information for our teams to blind-call the women and men posting the ads. We pull information and place it into a shared database that helps us track our calls and identifies duplicate advertisements. Based on the pictures posted we also flag and report to law enforcement anyone who looks underage.

When we call, we use a script and if no one answers, we leave a voicemail (if one is available) that includes a brief prayer. We follow up with an immediate text using template language, letting them know they're loved, cherished, and prayed for, and we give our contact information if they need help.

In case you're wondering, we never use our personal cell numbers; rather, we have a hotline number that's run through the ministry that we're able to access through an app. If a local call center exists we partner with them, and if not, we facilitate one the week of the game. We never want to duplicate services.

Technology Gone Bad

Minneapolis, Minnesota, 2018. The weather was so cold at this year's venue that it was more difficult to find girls who were being trafficked. Most of the trafficking was taking place inside, behind closed doors or at parties that cost thousands of dollars to get in the door. There were no outdoor "workers" because of the dangerously cold conditions, so we ramped up online outreach compared to years past. I was assigned to go online and research information/advertisements and place their demographic information into our database for our 24-hour call center to contact them.

As I scrolled through hundreds of ads, each had explicit photographs of nude girls being posted online for the taking. It was heartbreaking to see how many were posted and to think they were either being forced to do this by their pimp or, because of life circumstances, they feel like selling themselves is their only option to live.

Bow your heads with us and pray for every person, no matter their age, gender, or race, who has pornographic photographs online for the purposes of selling sexual services. Pray for divine intervention for each of the victims and for any person, man or woman, who is using technology to pimp and exploit God's children. Pray for these wicked website domain hosts that the Lord will right now lock up the technology, cause them to malfunction, and permanently shut them down. Pray for the cases against the major website, backpage.com, and for justice to be served for the thousands of children, men, and women trafficked on their site that the indictment said made more than $500 million in "prostitution-related revenue."

Also, keep in prayer every volunteer who conducts the online research to gather the information so we can contact those being exploited. Pray that God will put a shield over their mind and guard them against any ill effects of viewing the pornographic advertisements.

The Telephone of Light and Life

In 2018 I was part of a mission trip with more than 50 volunteers who went to one of football's largest sporting events in my home state of Minnesota. While there we researched online ads where pimps upload pictures of their victims. We collected the women's information from these sites so we could contact them through a call center to let them know we cared and could help them out of their situation. As the week progressed, it was amazing to see how essential this call center was to the rescues we facilitated.

During the calls, the women would sometimes answer and other times the pimp would. Sometimes the women wanted help and other times they would tell us it was their "choice." Each situation was completely different, yet strikingly the same.

Pray that God's healing light will shine to offer these women a true choice for freedom, allowing them to find a different path leading to a life of joy with no shame or condemnation.

Annual Collaborator

As the founder of Sufficient Grace Outreach, I've been involved in call outreach the week of the national football championship game for 7 years. Our outreach efforts in 2018 were very different thanks to the Skyway Railroad connecting different teams so we wouldn't overlap and duplicate calls.

Instead of each of the ministries pulling ads and calling separately, we created a shared database and everyone helped pull ads from backpage.com. All the teams worked together for the same goal of rescuing victims of sex trafficking the week of the game. As a result of the collaboration, Sufficient Grace's reach went well beyond our ministry's individual capacity in prior years. Collectively our teams researched more than 1800 ads to the glory of God. Our methodology in collecting shared data was a team effort and very humbling to be a part of.

Sufficient Grace's call center has historically made calls from North Carolina where we are headquartered, but in 2019 we plan on taking a team to Atlanta, Georgia to help with call outreach on site the week of the game.

Pray that we are able to continue extending our reach by working as partners in the service of our Lord, and that our resources multiply to help these women, children, and men.

The Final Call

Minneapolis, Minnesota 2018. I experienced many challenging situations during our outreach to those being trafficked the week of a major sporting event. My eyes were opened to some very difficult things I never thought could even exist. I spent a lot of time in the call center where I looked up online ads and put their information in our database. I also made outgoing calls.

The first shift I volunteered at the center was impactful. Initially, I was very hesitant to make calls and check for ads because those things were way beyond my comfort zone. At the end of my first shift, with about 10 minutes left, I thought, "Oh, that's good enough. I've already called so many people and it's almost time for bed, so that's good enough." Scrolling past a name on the list, I felt a tugging in my heart to call a particular number. I wrestled back and forth but eventually decided if I felt so strongly about calling the number, there must have been a reason.

I felt God telling me: "This isn't about you...this is about them." That message changed my whole perspective for the rest of the trip and still impacts me today. When I made the last call, a woman answered the phone and she was shocked when I asked if I could pray for her. Only God knows what was going on at that particular time God burdened me to contact her. She asked me to call back the next morning.

A teammate called her back and we offered her the help she needed. I am so glad I listened to my conviction and made that last call. My few short hours of discomfort in the call center were nothing compared to the lifetime of discomfort these women have lived through.

Pause and pray for this woman who received prayer and resources. What a great last call.

Someone's Daughter

Coming into the call center for the second morning of outreach I was excited to get another day going. When I looked at the call list, I thought, "It's going to be an easy day because we got most of it done the day before." I was quickly proven wrong. There were so many more numbers added throughout the night.

I realized, "These are someone's children." I wanted them all to respond and know we were there to help, but that's only in a perfect world. I was expectant and ready to see what God would do next.

Even though many calls and texts didn't have a response, please pray for each person who received our message of hope. If we made 1,000 calls and only one responded, it was all worth it.

CHAPTER 8
DIVINE CONNECTIONS

Unlikely Worship

Our team was conducting outreach in San Francisco's neighborhood called The Tenderloin District. We parked our van on one block and immediately felt an intense weight of darkness all around us. After parking, we began to war in the Spirit realm.

Our team spent more than an hour in just one spot, knowing there were many hurting people outside in great need of healing. It was an experience I'll never forget. We took turns getting out of the van in teams of three and four people and prayed for people on the street, while everyone in the van interceded.

We left that spot and made our way to a strip club destination plotted on our route. When we arrived, we couldn't find the entrance and the building was locked. We walked further down the street and suddenly live worship music filled the streets. A worship team was practicing right next to the club we were attempting to enter. We tried to gain access to where they were practicing, but a gate locked us out.

Someone who lived on the premises came home and we instantly clicked. We explained who we were and our purpose and asked if we could come in and worship with them. What took place next was nothing short of the glory of God falling on that place.

While it may have been an ordinary night of worship practice, the encounter for our team was divine. We needed refueling after praying and laying hands on those bound in severe mental illness, addiction, physical infirmities of all kinds, and prostitution.

I had volunteers in the van who were waiting outside come in so we could all worship together. We laid on the floor of that church and worshiped together for what felt like hours. As they practiced, our large team entered and, while they had no idea who we were until after worship, our spirits brought the heavens down. It was truly uninhibited worship.

We worked with this amazing ministry the rest of our trip and even trained a few of them in strip club outreach. We took them to the club next to their sanctuary and they connected with the owners. We found out after going inside that it wasn't a strip club. It was a sex club.

Essentially, people pay to go into the establishment and have sex throughout the large multi-floor building—some in the wide open for others to watch and some in more secluded areas. It was the most sadistic, masochistic place our team had ever witnessed. Statues of false gods were all over the place, televisions covered every wall with pornographic videos playing, along with other items too graphic to describe. Even writing about this place brings a heavy dark reminder.

Would you stop right now and pray for the owners of this place and those who enter? Also for the ministry which, when we went, literally shared a wall with this place?

We still have relationships with this ministry and after we left, they even helped Baby Rose's mom (see her testimony under the "Fighting Through Barriers" chapter) when she still needed help. They are reaching people and going places where others would never step foot: San Francisco City Impact. Amazing ministry and an amazing impact, to the glory of God!

Tattoo in Rock Bottom Cafe

It was so cold in Minneapolis that our team of three who were doing street outreach downtown stopped at Rock Bottom Cafe to warm up and get a quick bite to eat. My spirits were down as it was so much harder than past years to find and minister to the girls because the cold was keeping them from being on the streets. They were all indoors.

A ministry from Chicago, Ink 180, was with our team that evening. This ministry removes and does cover-ups for gang tattoos and tattoos placed on victims by their pimps. They also do tattoos to cover up wounds and scars caused by self-harm. I'd been praying for weeks that we would find a woman who'd benefit from his ministry. It was the end of the night. We were cold and had just finished grabbing a bite to eat. We were leaving the restaurant, ready to go back to the hotel.

One of the women on our team needed to use the restroom so we waited by the hostess area where we saw a woman sitting on a bench. I struck up a casual conversation with her and she asked me if we were "Chasers" of this major sporting event. I didn't quite understand what she was asking and she clarified, asking if we went to the game every year as "chasers." I let her know our purpose and she gasped in disbelief.

She was waiting at Rock Bottom Cafe for a few girls who were being trafficked. She was helping victims because she was trafficked 30 years prior, in the 80s.

Just then I saw the founder of Ink 180 and was reminded of his gift. I asked the woman, "Do you have any tattoos that your trafficker put on you?"

She instantly blurted out, "YES." Tears came to her eyes, as she proceeded to pull her shirt off her shoulder.

Thirty years before this encounter her trafficker tattooed a name and gang symbol on her shoulder. With tears streaming down her face, she described how every single day she had a visual reminder of the horrors that happened to her. I asked if she wanted to get it removed and introduced her to Ink 180's ministry founder. She fell crying on my chest and shook for at least 20 minutes.

The next day we met and Ink 180 was able to remove the tattoo in less than 20 minutes. She will no longer have to look at the visual reminder. To say she was grateful is an understatement. She asked us to take pictures and a video of it being removed and allowed the Skyway Railroad and Ink 180 to also post her story on social media. This amazing testimony is on our Facebook page.

Stop and pray for this woman, as God uses her to reach those who are being trafficked. Pray for her continued financial stability and direction from God. And say a prayer for Ink 180, for God to continue using their ministry to help those with permanent reminders of their trauma and for financial provision to provide their services without charge.

Full Circle

We stood in a large circle praying after our daily de-briefing and were getting ready to break into our outreach teams. Someone was fervently praying and the room erupted in warfare prayer. The presence of the Lord filled the room in such a tangible way.

I opened my eyes to see whose anointed prayer invaded heaven and what I witnessed next was nothing short of a miracle. The woman praying was a graduate of a recovery program I was the director of years before. She came to the center straight from jail, broken and insecure.

Here she was years later (a successful graduate and Chicago Masters Commission student) powerfully interceding for those we would encounter who desperately needed a touch from Jesus, just like she did years before.

I lost it. Tears streamed down my face in utter gratitude and awe. What a privilege to serve alongside a woman who years prior I taught and counseled during her most vulnerable time. To see her come full circle and be part of a team who reached and rescued women is what our mission is all about. Jen you are inspiration to many.

Pray now, with me, that we may encounter and impact many more Jens, neglected, abused, and stolen by the darkness; and that we may bring them the saving light of God's grace.

CHAPTER 9
RESCUES

Law Enforcement Collaboration

On our first official day after training, I had the privilege of spending time with a woman and her son who were rescued as a result of the call center. Weeks after the outreach event, I'm still in touch with her. It was and still is incredible to hear her story and be God's love to her.

The team was able to help her and many other survivors find an apartment and get a good job. I had the honor of looking into the eyes of these women and loving them for who they were. I was able to be gracious to them, to be kindness to them, to be a listening ear and a shoulder to cry on. Although the work we did was emotionally draining, it was incredibly rewarding.

On the third day of our hands-on work, we had an amazing breakthrough. Many victims were reaching out to the call center, wanting to be rescued from the lifestyle. They were trying to get away from their pimp and to a safe location; however, it was difficult.

There was one potential rescue who was texting the call center number and, because of safety, we felt the best option was to bring in law enforcement. Based on her texts she was not safe and couldn't get away from her pimp. Her texts were filled with anxiety and she described having to delete them as soon as she sent them so her trafficker would not see them.

I had the opportunity to create a document for law enforcement delineating all of our contact with this distressed victim so they could get a clear understanding of the situation. What happened next you wouldn't believe!

Not only did law enforcement get the mother and her children to safety, they tracked her pimp to a hotel operation and shut the whole thing down, rescuing many other women and their children. Unbelievable! Only God can do that! Praise Him!

We know rescue is just the first step in a long restoration process. Please stop and pray for this woman and her child and all the others who were reported rescued because of this brave woman's actions. Also pray for justice, as the traffickers were arrested.

Changed Perspective

Starting this trip I wasn't really expecting much. Even though I knew some or most of the girls didn't choose this life, I thought when we offered a way out, they wouldn't want help or they would think it was a scam. I was quickly put in my place. Within the first several hours we rescued two women.

As soon as the rescued women were brought in I was part of a team who went online and looked for resources. We called a number of churches and programs to see who could house or have space for a mother and child. They all had nothing. They didn't even express an interest in what we were doing. It really opened my eyes to see how narrow-minded people can be. It just broke my heart but didn't crush my spirit.

We kept pushing. I've never felt so united with a team of people on a mission trip who I've never met. God really moved and did great things.

Rescuing is only the first step in our efforts because we know the victims have to choose to make difficult decisions and remain on the road to recovery with so many barriers. We provided options to those we rescued, but, unfortunately, some chose not to follow through and the next day we saw their ads back online.

Please stop and pray for every woman we rescued at the major sporting events, for them to continue taking difficult and brave steps on their road to recovery.

From Rescue to Placement

I had the opportunity to go on one of the first rescues. It was my first time going out so I didn't know what to expect. After picking the women up, our team drove them to a destination. I suddenly realized, "This is a 'normal' person." She was polite, friendly, and engaged in the conversation. I know that may sound strange, but I realized I had a certain expectation/classification of the women. That day I was able to see how wrong I was in my thinking and judgment.

I had the opportunity to go where she was staying and secure all of her belongings, most of which were in garbage bags. I was amazed to see how God moved when all options seemed lost. How incredible to be there with this woman from the beginning when we rescued her, to the end when she was placed. I truly felt like I helped to change someone's life. These are moments I will never forget.

Please stop and say a prayer for this woman whom the team was able to help get out of the industry and into her own apartment.

Bar of Neutrogena Soap

I had an amazing encounter with a pastor who was a volunteer on one of our teams. He volunteered in previous years through a non-profit that facilitated a Prayer Bowl where he interceded from home. This year, 2018, was the first year he actually came to the venue to do outreach with us.

The pastor was in school and didn't think he would be able to attend the outreach, but he felt something telling him he needed to be there on the ground. He went to his professor who granted him permission to miss the class so he could participate. Before leaving, someone gave him a bar of Neutrogena soap and told him he was supposed to give it away during his trip to a specific person. As he drove to the venue, he saw a vision of women washing their faces and when they looked in the mirror they saw Jesus' reflection.

When he arrived at the venue he gave the bar of soap to one of the women volunteers who was going on night outreach and shared his experience. The volunteer in turn came to the hotel where we were staying, handed me the bar of soap, and explained the story. I immediately knew who the soap was for.

Earlier in the day, I was asked to go to the probation department with a rescue who had a pending trial and was assigned a probation officer. I worked in juvenile probation for 14 years in Chicago so I had experience in this area. When debriefed I was told she had a male probation officer who wasn't being very friendly to the advocate on the phone and the woman needed to go do a weekly drug drop.

When I went to meet with the probation officer he wasn't there but we were able to meet with his partner, a woman. It became apparent the woman we rescued felt more comfortable opening up with the female officer and I immediately recognized the victim had difficulty (for obvious reasons) working with men. We were able to identify this during our meeting and I requested that a supervisor consider assigning her to a female officer because of her history of being exploited and trafficked by men.

We spent half the day together and I got to know this woman who was rescued from backpage.com through the call center. She had an atrocious life. At the age of 13, she was sold by her own mother to her aunt who'd recently married a man from Saudi Arabia. She was then taken there to live, and described having to dress up and dance in front of men.

During our conversation, I commented on her beautiful hair when she took it down from the sloppy wrapped-up bun on top of her head. She described cutting it all off when she was a child living in Saudi Arabia and forced to dress up and dance in front of men. She didn't want to be attractive to them.

Her family was planning to sell her to one of the men for considerable money as a form of prearranged marriage. During parts of our conversation it was difficult to understand all the details but somehow she escaped and came back to the U.S.

When I asked about her father, she said he was a pimp and so was his father–her grandfather. Trafficking was deep in her lineage. She was trafficked again at the age of 18 by non-family members. At the time we rescued her, she was tough as nails and said she put her own self on backpage.com.

At the beginning of our first encounter, I started out praying with her. At the conclusion of my prayer, she did something I've never experienced in my 20 years of outreach. She grabbed my hands as I was letting go and began praying herself–hard, fervently, and sincerely. I had my eyes open and was in awe. Later in the week when I brought up her prayer, she joked and said, "I had to keep praying because you didn't get everything. You missed some things." I and another volunteer chuckled.

So back to the bar of soap…when the volunteer came to me and gave me the bar of soap and told me the story behind it, I immediately knew it was for this woman who was rescued. I could've easily given the woman the bar of soap and explained how the pastor got it and the vision he had when driving, but it wasn't my soap to give.

The pastor agreed to meet with me and the female volunteer in the hotel hallway and give it to the survivor. He stood before her and began sharing about the bar of soap. How God was able to wash everything from her and that when she looked in the mirror he prayed she'd see the reflection of Jesus.

The woman's face was hardened but you could tell by her body language it was taking everything in her to not let tears burst from her eyes. She had so many walls up when it came to men.

The female volunteer with me began speaking and immediately the survivor broke down in tears. We pointed out, with the pastor there, our observation of the woman being very guarded with men— and for good reason. Our prayer was for God to allow healing to take place so she could experience godly encounters with men, like this pastor, who had no motives or ill will.

Would you stop and pray for this woman right now...for her family, for her physical and mental health (she had a traumatic brain injury which caused her to forget things and get disoriented), for healing from all the trauma she has endured, and for her pending court case?

CHAPTER 10
MYTHS SHATTERED

One of the goals of this book is to shatter the myths so many believe about the atrocity of human trafficking. As you've seen in some of the reflections, some of the volunteers who came for the first time, came with misconceptions that were shattered after their firsthand experiences.

At six years old a child doesn't have a dream of growing up and being a prostitute. Many, however, ask why a girl being trafficked or prostituted doesn't "just leave." It's not that simple. Most of our every day "normal" pales in comparison to their everyday "normal."

Traffickers target and groom their victims. They often prey on vulnerable girls who aren't a "liability," meaning no one will come looking for them—for instance, girls who are in the foster care system or who come from broken homes. These children sadly don't have a parent who notices or advocates when they're missing. And children lured into the lifestyle are often sent to recruit other children in the foster care system. During my tenure working in juvenile court, many girls living in group homes recruited other girls in the home to run away and they brought them to the trafficking ring.

Other situations would also probably surprise you. Some victims come from good homes but got mixed in with the wrong people. Slowly but surely they find themselves sucked into a lifestyle they never imagined they'd live. Much manipulation, grooming, and fear is instilled in these girls. They're told if they leave or tell anyone that the traffickers know where their families live and they'll harm or kill them. They've personally witnessed and been subjected to their trafficker's violence so the victims know the threats aren't shallow.

On the outside looking in, it may be tempting to believe the myth that these girls and boys have a "choice." Yet, for most the alternatives to their reality usually have insurmountable barriers to reach freedom. I can't tell you the number of rescues who say they're "working" to put food on the table, to keep a roof over their heads, to provide for their children, and yes, to sometimes meet an addiction most were introduced to through their traffickers as a means to keep them bound.

Following are a few atypical encounters we had at the championship game outreach that goes against the typical stereotypes society labels prostitutes.

Berkeley Student Loans

In San Francisco at the sporting event outreach in 2016, we enter a strip club. Caucasian girls were walking around completely unclothed, apparently feeling natural in this environment. Several of us approached one girl, whom we will call Emily, and handed her a rose. We told her how we go every year to the venue where the national football game is hosted, and we wanted to share how she was beautiful and filled with great purpose. Emily asked what she owed us for the flower and I told her, "It's free."

She and the other girls in the club were blown away by our love and willingness to come and encourage them. Emily, in particular, had tears in her eyes. She expressed how nice we were to come in the strip club and how our brief encounter made her night.

We learned how she started working at the strip club because after graduating from Berkeley she became a counselor but couldn't afford her student loan payments on the salary she was making. So she began "stripping" to pay back her loans.

Emily and her friend had gone to church together and they asked if we could pray for them. So right there, in the middle of this strip club, with men looking on and other strippers working the floor, four of us stood and prayed for their future, their finances, and their faith.

Not all who enter in the industry fit what you may stereotypically think. In 2018, UC Berkeley was ranked #21 in the United States and only enrolls the best of the best. Emily was a college educated graduate from one of the finest institutions in America, just trying to make ends meet. How Satan lies and deceives God's precious children. Stop and say a prayer for these beautiful women of God.

Mother in College with an Autistic Child

2018, Minneapolis. The weather was freezing cold. I was in the car thinking, "Who on the commission that decides where these games are hosted voted to have the championship game in Minneapolis during the first weekend in February?" I volunteered in three other venues where this annual event was hosted and this year was so different because of the cold.

Our team on this night was assigned to conduct outreach in strip clubs. It was early in the week so our teams hadn't gone to every club yet. We had just left a strip club where we successfully gained entry. The navigator on the team gave the address to the next location a few short miles away. Once we got there, we determined after looking at the notes in our outreach spreadsheet that a team had already gone to that club earlier in the week.

As the team leader, I decided we'd make sure we went to every club on our itinerary first before we went back to the same clubs multiple times. We, therefore, decided not to enter that club. Even though we had no intention of going inside and went there by "mistake," God doesn't make mistakes! He has a history of taking us off our scheduled stop to divinely meet and minister to someone. Such was the case that night.

We pulled over in the club parking lot looking for the address of the next club we would go to. Next to our parked vehicle was a girl who looked like she'd just gotten off work at the club. I jumped out of the car into the frigid cold and approached her car window, praying the entire time, because in this day in age there's no telling what can happen if you walk up to a vehicle and tap on someone's window.

Thankfully she rolled it down partially and I introduced myself, told her how we saw her sitting in her car and wanted to know if she needed prayer. She immediately rolled the window all the way down, apparently not caring about the cold air that would penetrate into her heart.

I quickly learned she knew the Lord. She went to church and knew the Word of God. From the onset of our interaction she immediately broke down, and after we asked if she was safe (the first question we ask every girl), she shared how she worked as a stripper "by choice" and wasn't being "pimped" or "prostituted."

This is a typical response we often hear from girls working in the industry. What a deceiving lie of the enemy. Every girl working in a strip club is sexually exploited by the establishments who charge the girl for each lap dance she gives and requires a certain quota for the evening. But I digress.

This woman, whom I will name Victoria, worked a regular job during the day, was in college, and also worked at the strip club in the evening to help provide for her children, one of whom was 11 years old and autistic.

I asked what specifically she wanted me to pray for and she told me about her job interview the following week at an agency—get this—that advocates for autistic children where she would make $50,000. At that rate she would be able to quit working at the strip club and do something she was called to do. Just speaking about helping autistic children brought tears streaming down her face because she wanted to help others in similar situations.

As my shivering hands were clutched in her perfectly manicured hands, tears streamed down her face. We prayed the fire of God to go before her in that job interview and for God to supernaturally open doors for her to walk through. Mid-prayer she dropped my hands, raised them in the air and I laid hands on her mind and prayed against any anxiety, fear, doubt, rejection, and fear. She literally called out Scripture over her mind with her hands raised to the roof of the car.

Victoria so desperately wanted out and that night, while we were not supposed to be there, God saw otherwise. I got back in the car, while cold physically, on fire spiritually as a result of this God-ordained appointment that I will carry with me for the rest of my life. What a beautiful and brave single mother. Stop and pray for Victoria and her autistic son however the Spirit leads you.

Widowed Single Mom

It was our first day of outreach in Minneapolis, 2018, and I was working the 7 a.m. to 7 p.m. shift at our call center. We had a team who looked up ads on various websites known for girls being trafficked or exploited online, and they placed this contact information in our database.

Most of the calls I made resulted in me leaving a voice message for the women, but on rare occasions, some did answer. When they heard the first few words from our script, they unfortunately often hung up. We also followed up with a text and this was where we got most responses from women who wanted our help.

That night I got a chance to talk to one of the women during an outgoing phone call who asked for help. When I spoke to her she told me that her husband had passed away a year ago and it had been difficult for her to take care of her daughter while paying all her bills. She spoke of wanting out of "this life."

It's in these small moments that our team was reminded that people don't want this lifestyle but feel they have no other options in providing for their kids. God, we join hands in the spiritual realm with every reader right now and ask that You would touch this woman and her child and every other woman who feels trapped in sexual exploitation as the only means of providing for their family. Open doors only You can and provide a safe and permanent exit. Comfort this single widowed mother in the grief of losing her husband.

CHAPTER 11
FIGHTING THROUGH BARRIERS

After conducting outreach for more than a decade, I've seen firsthand the barriers trafficking victims encounter. There are the obvious barriers of being extracted from the control of their pimp and remaining safe. But there are also psychological barriers to overcome. Captivity normally doesn't take place overnight. Human trafficking victims are carefully groomed, manipulated, and tortured physically, mentally, and emotionally. And trafficking isn't just something taking place in other countries or only in our urban cities in America. It exists in every community and every setting-rural and urban.

Sadly the barriers survivors encounter once rescued are often just as hard for them to navigate as the realities they endured with their trafficker. And that's often why they stay bound.

We do not judge, we do not criticize, we do not shove Jesus and religion down their throat. We are called simply to love, meet each person where they are, and display Christ in all our interactions.

One of the main barriers for victims trying to leave their trafficker is the extreme shortage of housing, especially for the specific needs of those trafficked. Women with children face even greater barriers to finding housing. Unfortunately, many trafficking victims end up in homeless shelters which are ill-equipped to handle the level of care survivors need.

Trafficking victims sustain a plethora of trauma. Having managed a human trafficking safe house for years, I've seen the night tremors and frequent flashbacks. These victims are in dire need of not just traditional therapy but trauma-informed interventions for which there are little to no resources. And when resources do exist in the community, small nonprofits usually cannot afford to provide the therapy hours needed.

After attending sporting events and seeing the huge shortage of beds compared to the number of women needing placement, one of our strategies is to form a national partnership of small Christian safe houses around the country. During the week of the championship game, we have relationships with safe houses across the country, allowing us to place rescues nationally.

During the year leading up to the game, we begin partnering with organizations already conducting outreach, so when we leave the ministry will continue. Knowing we will be in the venue only the week of the game, we always want to build upon the good work already taking place in a city and help them with the increase in volume the week of the game by providing already trained volunteers to help in their efforts.

The best local responses and coordinated care we encountered at the annual football championship outreach was in Phoenix, Arizona, in 2015. We were able to provide leadership and volunteers to operate a temporary shelter specializing in working with human trafficking rescues the week of the event. From the shelter, teams worked to place those rescued into coordinated long-term care locally and nationally. The city had existing outreach ministries and teams with established routes and relationships. Our volunteers were able to come alongside these existing ministries and help.

Our annual outreach in San Francisco regrettably had the worst access to resources we've experienced. Prior to the game, we attempted to find a ministry to come alongside, but could find no one doing outreach to those being trafficked. When we got there and began conducting outreach, the women were shocked. They had never seen anyone come into the venues in which they were working. When we did rescue victims, unfortunately there were limited housing resources.

In addition to housing barriers keeping many victims bound in human trafficking, many are involved in court proceedings, either through criminal court or through their state's department of children and family services (DCS) for abuse or neglect cases involving their children. With pending court cases it's often difficult for them to leave the city, much less the state, to another jurisdiction where freedom is being offered. We've had many conversations with probation officers, DCS workers, and court systems to try and help advocate for removal from the victims' triggers and danger.

Something else we encounter a lot is victims have children with their trafficker. We are even starting to see women intentionally being impregnated by their pimp as a means of controlling them through the bloodline of their child. The mother can't leave the state and often feels financially and emotionally dependent on her trafficker.

Pimps also control their workers by confiscating their identification. We've rescued girls who need to get home or want to relocate to one of our networked safe houses; however, they don't have their required ID to get on an airplane. Their pimp has taken it. We have the vision to have a private jet on standby at the football championship game in case we have a rescue who needs relocation and cannot travel because they have no identification. We've learned of ministries in the U.S. that partner with private pilots who donate their time to help transport these victims to safety.

Another barrier for many victims we rescue is the need for detox before they can be placed. Many victims have been doped up on drugs by their trafficker. They then become addicted, and are dependent on the trafficker to maintain their high. When they reach the point of wanting out, many jurisdictions have a shortage of detox facilities for those with no insurance.

In addition, we've encountered barriers when a person finishes detox successfully and within a certain amount of days try to return but are denied. Patients are often only allowed to enter detox once in a certain amount of days (e.g., every 30 days) because of insurance. Therefore, if they relapse they will stay on the streets because help wasn't available after they fell back into temptation.

The biggest barrier we see—no matter where we conduct outreach—is the shortage of quality housing and sustainable jobs. Many survivors have children, which increases the difficulty of finding housing and employment because many programs don't allow children and if they do, the mother needs childcare while they work.

Our goal is to help advocate and navigate these barriers with tenacity and resolve. When we've been successful in relocating survivors, we've seen tremendous testimonies of starting over. Even when barriers keep bound those we reach, we remain steadfast, consistent voices in their lives. We still keep in touch via social media and text with some women we encountered years ago at sporting events. We've seen some of them spiral deeper into challenges because of a lack of resources and personal resolve, but we remain present and prayerful that they will make the courageous decision to exit bondage.

The following are a few encounters at a championship game where barriers and obstacles plagued our interactions.

Baby Rose

Oakland, California, 2016. We were conducting street outreach and saw a young pregnant girl on the corner getting in and out of cars. She saw us giving roses throughout the week and after several nights, she agreed to come with our night outreach team to get something to eat.

She was literally starving and filled her plate several times. We learned she was seven months pregnant and hadn't received any prenatal care. She agreed to go with us to the hospital. The team who rescued her was named Rose of Sharon and about eight of our people huddled around this beautiful young woman in the ER when the doctor wheeled in an ultrasound machine.

It was like all of us were becoming godparents at that moment and the doctor informed us that the baby was a girl. Someone in the room shouted out "Baby Rose" (after the name of the outreach ministry).

Our next challenge was finding her a place that allowed pregnant women, a huge barrier. The San Francisco Bay area had very few shelters, but one of our fearless placement coordinators after making hundreds of calls found a place that would accept her. However, she had to admit to being trafficked, something that most will not readily admit upon first encounters. She denied any involvement so that placement did not work.

A juvenile probation officer specializing in minors who are sex trafficked in Chicago also spent hours making a plethora of phone calls attempting to find a place. We finally found one and drove her to the long-term shelter about 30 or 40 minutes away. Leaving her that day was difficult for our team.

Unfortunately, she later left the shelter and returned to the streets but to this day, she keeps in touch with several of our team members. We learned throughout the few years we've worked with her that she also had two older children who were in child protective custody.

She had her baby and, much to our surprise, baby Rose was a boy! Since that major sporting event, she had another baby and asked several times for help to be placed in a program. She never followed through and has never admitted to being trafficked, despite our team witnessing it on the streets and all the signs being present.

She has learned to survive and has very little trust, and for great reason. In 2018 when I wrote this testimony from years prior I messaged this young woman on social media and learned she had just found out that week she was pregnant again.

Would you stop and pause right now and pray for this precious young woman and her children?

Ocean's Deep

While in Phoenix, Arizona, in 2015 we partnered with the Phoenix Dream Center who provided a quality shelter care facility open 24 hours a day with specialized care for the women rescued. I'll never forget one woman who was rescued and placed in the temporary shelter. She battled all week to stay positive and became very attached to our team. Through the diligence of all involved, we found a placement for her in Atlanta, Georgia. She was determined to leave Phoenix and all that she'd endured. However, she didn't have an ID.

I got on the phone with my pastor back in Chicago and told him I needed a private jet to get this woman from Phoenix to Atlanta. He began calling his connections and someone he knew in California had a private plane. Unfortunately, his plane was overseas so it wasn't available.

After a lot of research, we determined the only way we could get her to Atlanta was by Greyhound. One of our staff in Chicago created an ID card with our organization name on it and emailed it to me. I took it to FexEx to have it printed and laminated.

The time came for her to leave. On the way to the Greyhound station, we stopped at the airport to drop off others who had volunteered all week with us. We were all jam-packed in a van with this rescued woman, and Hillsong United's song "Oceans" came on the radio. An all–out worship band busted out in that van. It was truly angelic at times, and off-key and loud at others. It's as if we were screaming this song over her life. She was in awe and spoke of never seeing so many women filled with joy, love, and compassion.

We got out at the Greyhound station and I went in to purchase her ticket. Everything was automated on a touch screen pad on which we entered her starting and ending point. After I paid, the machine began spitting out ticket after ticket after ticket. In total, she had to transfer nine times to get to her destination.

All of a sudden panic came upon her. Her hands were shaking and she began saying she couldn't do it. "How am I going to know what ticket to use? How am I going to know how to transfer? I'm gonna get lost. What if I lose a ticket and get stranded somewhere I don't know anyone?" We stopped, laid hands on her, and prayed the peace of God upon her. Honestly, seeing the nine tickets overwhelmed me. I can't imagine the anxiety she felt with the added pressure of so many unknowns.

I took the nine tickets plus the receipt and put them in order so she would know which one to use first, second, third, and so on. Then I put a number on the corner of each one in case she got them out of order. I also bought her a pre-paid Visa card so she could make calls and get food along the journey.

We stayed with her until she boarded. What a brave woman! She finished the program we placed her in, and one of our volunteers, who is a probation officer in Chicago and volunteered that year at the shelter, has kept in touch with her to this day. Years later she's still in Atlanta and guess what? She is married and doing great!

Pause and pray for this woman's continued success and all the women who encountered barriers by not having their IDs to get away from their traffickers.

Where's the Church?

We rescued a woman and her four-year-old son one day on our first official day of outreach. I began contacting local churches to see if they could help this single mom in any way. I was sad and honestly frustrated that churches would transfer or connect me with local government services or simply tell me they couldn't help for a variety of other reasons (e.g., they used up their benevolence funds, they only help shelter people in June, they don't help with local ministry...only missions).

I was left heartbroken, knowing this particular city's church community didn't have much set up to help people in need of shelter. Having come from a very active urban church in one of our country's largest cities, the apathy of these churches was eye-opening for me.

Here we are from ministries all around the country, coming to this city to help be the hands and feet of Jesus and we have an actual person sitting in front of us with real needs. Needs that biblically we are called to stand alongside. Yet, the local churches didn't have open arms to welcome this one family.

Join us right now in praying for God's bride nationally, to not fall asleep but rather be the voice in the wilderness to the broken, battered, and bruised in their cities. And pray that God will give strength and favor to the many churches who are heeding the call to reach, rescue, and restore the lost for God's eternal glory! Church of Jesus Christ, we hold the keys to the kingdom of heaven. Let's be ready.

Rescued Into the Shallow

Minneapolis, Minnesota, 2018. One of the sad things about rescuing those being trafficked is that there are barely any programs, resources, or homes for these women to go into once they are rescued. We called more than 60 churches, community centers, and local nonprofits to ask for help—either financially or with housing for one rescue. Not one of them helped us.

We relentlessly continued advocating and, of course, God came through and the victims were all safely placed. However, my heart just broke for those in the future who wanted to be rescued but there are no resources available to them. It took a team with experience, perseverance, connections, and tenacity to place some of the rescued women.

Please continue to pray for the increase of housing opportunities and healing programs, as there are little to none in most places, especially for pregnant and parenting mothers.

CHAPTER 12
RAISING AWARENESS

We always engage in some type of awareness campaigns to educate people attending the annual championship football game about what takes place with individuals being trafficked. We leave awareness items in bathrooms (magnets) and around the city. We also provide cards to fans with our information.

It's always amazing to meet people who think human trafficking takes place only in other countries. Most also have no idea that the week they're celebrating their national football team is the single highest time for trafficking. Once educated, they all acknowledge that it makes total sense because of the volume of men celebrating, partying, and creating a high demand for escort services.

The awareness items we leave in various locations are also designed to provide a resource if and when people witness human trafficking taking place. The national human trafficking hotline number is displayed on each item, as well as local hotline numbers for people to contact if they see something suspicious.

Every year we bring a group of Master's Commission students from Chicago, many of whom are part of the awareness outreach teams. Chicago Master's Commission is a college of higher learning, offering eight different AA and BA degree options through West Coast Bible College and Seminary. The students all participate in a mission trip, with our annual outreach offered as one option. The following are some reflections of volunteers participating on awareness outreach teams.

Ten Minutes Changed Travel Perspective

San Francisco Airport, 2016. With other team members I spent 12 hours in the baggage claim and surrounding areas within the airport terminals. After an extended time, airport security and TSA began noticing us and one TSA agent asked what we were doing handing out all the roses to people. We explained our purpose and he was so grateful.

Another woman waiting in the airport also asked me what we were doing. When I informed her, she asked how we identified when someone was being trafficked. I explained that we attend training classes in how to recognize signs and, ultimately, if we provide resources during outreach to a person who wasn't being trafficked we met a goal of raising awareness by providing the information.

In only 10 minutes of sitting with her and sharing observations of people exiting the secure airport locations and into the baggage claim area, she was completely amazed. Within a short period of time, she was able to spot and identify girls who were potentially being trafficked, whereas previously she'd never paid attention.

Her career entailed a lot of traveling and for all the years she was in and out of airports, the signs were right under her nose and she never noticed them. She was too busy, like most of us, getting to her gate, securing her luggage, and rushing out the door to get her ride. She was accustomed to looking right past it, like so many others. When she stopped and paid attention just for a brief time, her eyes were opened to a world to which she was previously oblivious. Years after that encounter, I often wonder if her travels are still the same or if our 10-minute life lesson marked her forever.

Stop and pray now that more eyes become open to the atrocity of human trafficking happening right in front of them.

Mall of America

During one day of outreach in 2018, I was part of a team in Minneapolis, Minnesota, who was placing pre-made items designed to bring awareness to human trafficking taking place at this annual football event. To expose the realities, we left items at various parks and bus stops around the city. Our last stop was the Mall of America.

As you can imagine, security was extremely heightened during the week of the game. There is always an increased threat of terrorist attacks to structures with national recognition and massive amounts of patrons, especially during a week with the high international visibility that this game brings.

Before coming to the venue and during the event, we asked different people in authority at the Mall of America if we could place our pre-made items in bathrooms to raise awareness. We met with the Public Relations office and they said we couldn't. However, it was great to hear they were working with an anti-trafficking organization and all their staff was trained on how to notice signs. That gave us encouragement.

Pray for even greater awareness of this issue, as well as the signs of human trafficking. Call God's light to illuminate opportunities for all to work together to put an end to this cruel reality for so many.

Raising Awareness in the Darkness

In 2018 I was part of a team charged with raising awareness through setting out hand-painted pieces of wood with the word "love" on them. A sticker with a call center number was on the back for anyone who suspected something or if they were in a dangerous situation themselves.

Each night we had teams traveling for hours in each direction, placing blocks downtown in local cities, gas stations, and truck stops. Because many pimps stop at these places, we put the blocks in bathrooms so the women would hopefully see them and give us a call. We also handed out flyers at local events and talked with people to raise awareness. I was in shock to learn how many people didn't know human trafficking happened in the States or hadn't even heard of it.

After nine days on our mission trip in 2018, I was drained. I was completely and utterly exhausted. And if I'm honest, weeks out at the writing of this reflection, I'm still "coming to" because of all we witnessed. There's so much darkness in the world, but let me tell you, there's also a lot of goodness—goodness in Christ. There's so much hope in Him for which I'm grateful.

The survivors we rescued in Minneapolis are still recovering and many more need to be rescued. But we find peace knowing the needed healing will never come from any man. It can come only from our heavenly Father. We prayed over—and still are praying over—each bag, rose, tissue, flyer, and woman we came in contact with, specifically for God's will to be done through each of them.

Negative 13 Below Zero

We were in Minneapolis, Minnesota, at the end of January and beginning of February. The weather was 13 below with the wind-chill even colder. I was part of teams who put out awareness items all over the city. Even though it was cold, I placed them with joy because more people needed to know and more people needed to be saved.

At one point our team got together as a group and started praying for each other and for our minds and hearts to be protected because of everything we saw and witnessed. We asked the Holy Spirit to continue to be with us and keep blessing the team. His Spirit was poured out so thick and tangible. The trip was an eye-opener and a blessing.

As the trip came to an end I began to really have time to reflect and see how good God had been. During one assignment, I posted pictures and facts about human trafficking in the U.S. on social media. As I was doing research, it was crazy to see how people think trafficking is a myth at this sporting event. I just hope what we're doing raises more awareness and people will stop thinking this is stuff that just happens in the movies. It's real. We've seen it and our lives will forever be changed.

Please join us in praying for the powerful forces in the sports industry who don't want the bad publicity that human trafficking brings to their major annual football championship game. Instead of trying to cover it up or sweep it under the rug, we pray that they will partner with organizations like us to help combat it.

The Cost of Chasing the One

This year, 2018, has been a totally different year for me. I was able to go to Houston, Texas, last year so I had an idea of what to expect at this year's outreach. However, everything was different from my outlook before the trip started to when the actual outreach took place.

I talked to a friend back home during the trip and explained what we were doing. My friend said something simple, yet profound. He said, "The cost of chasing the one." That hit me and I really started to break that down.

All the time it took to prep for the trip, praying, fundraising, driving up to Minnesota, losing lots of sleep, giving up time to drive everyone where they needed to go, and countless other ways myself and this team sacrificed—these are the costs to be able to rescue just one woman. That would've been worth it, but we've been blessed to rescue many more than just one woman this year.

I can't even put into words what it feels like. This industry, these women, are NOT too far gone. They are not out of God's reach.

Pray now that we are blessed to continue to seek them out and help them find rescue.

ABOUT THE AUTHOR

The Skyway Railroad is a non-profit with a mission to unite Christian organizations nationally and collectively liberate those bound in targeted modern day slaveries:
Poverty, Addiction, Trafficking, Crime, Health (P.A.T.C.H.).

Our human trafficking efforts have both national and local impact in the greater Memphis, Tennessee Mid-South region. We disrupt sex trafficking through a local and national network of abolitionists who reach, rescue, and restore survivors. We provide safe passage and placement in a network of Christian safe houses nationally for rescued survivors who aren't safe in the jurisdiction where they've been trafficked. While pimps are coordinated nationally, we also can relocate survivors to a jurisdiction away from their trafficker through our coordinated efforts.

Every year the Skyway Railroad partners with the Chicago Masters Commission, Sufficient Grace, other non profits, and federal, state, and local law enforcement officials to reach, rescue, and safely place sex trafficking victims flown to the national football championship game.

Voices Outside the Stadium is a compilation of encounters our volunteers had when conducting outreach at the championship football game in venues known for human trafficking (strip clubs, bus and truck stops, brothels, massage parlors, etc.). Volunteers submitted reflections that were compiled and edited by Kaitrin Valencia.

One hundred percent of the proceeds from *Voices Outside the Stadium* fund the Skyway Railroad's annual outreach at the national football game, including outreach supplies, lodging, travel, and victim services and placement. Thank you for your investment.

If you want more information about our organization and ways you can support, please visit www.skywayrailroad.org and follow us on social media.

BEHIND THE COVER

The *Voices Outside the Stadium* cover has powerful meanings embedded throughout that we don't want to leave unspoken.

Those with a history of playing sports may recognize the chalkboard look of the X's and O's with arrows pointing where the play directs. These sports playbooks embedded throughout the cover represent our outreach taking place at major sporting events. While coaches have their playbooks inside the locker rooms before and during the football championship games, our teams also have logistical playbooks to reach, rescue, and place those trafficked. A tremendous amount of networking and preparation for the annual outreach transpires for a year or longer prior to the game.

Also, notice where the X's and O's are strategically placed (X over the woman's mouth to represent her silenced voice, O around "children" on back cover and take note of the word that arrow points to, and the XOXO on back cover which is often used as a symbol for hugs and kisses).

The background of the entire cover is a brown paper bag. Men bound in pornography often cover magazines with paper bags as a disguise so surrounding people won't know what contents are within.

Lastly, the woman depicted is dressed up, however, obviously numb with her identity masked. What's seen on the outside is not at all what we see on the inside.

Thank you Imelda Valencia Cuevas for your creativity and heart for this issue.

Made in the USA
San Bernardino, CA
15 December 2018